LIVING RICH
by
SPENDING
SMART

LIVING RICH
by
SPENDING
SMART

HOW TO GET MORE OF
WHAT YOU REALLY WANT

GREGORY KARP

Vice President, Publisher: Tim Moore
Associate Publisher and Director of Marketing: Amy Neidlinger
Executive Editor: Jim Boyd
Editorial Assistant: Pamela Boland
Development Editor: Russ Hall
Digital Marketing Manager: Julie Phifer
Marketing Coordinator: Megan Colvin
Cover Designer: John Barnett
Managing Editor: Gina Kanouse
Project Editor: Chelsey Marti
Copy Editor: Geneil Breeze
Proofreader: Leslie Joseph
Indexer: Lisa Stumpf
Compositor: Jake McFarland
Manufacturing Buyer: Dan Uhrig

FT Press offers excellent discounts on this book when ordered in quantity for bulk purchases
or special sales. For more information, please contact U.S. Corporate and Government Sales,
1-800-382-3419, corpsales@pearsontechgroup.com. For sales outside the U.S., please contact
International Sales at international@pearsoned.com.

Printed in the United States of America

Third Printing April 2008

ISBN-10   0-13-235009-2

ISBN-13   978-0-13-235009-9

Pearson Education LTD.
Pearson Education Australia PTY, Limited.
Pearson Education Singapore, Pte. Ltd.
Pearson Education North Asia, Ltd.
Pearson Education Canada, Ltd.
Pearson Educatión de Mexico, S.A. de C.V.
Pearson Education—Japan
Pearson Education Malaysia, Pte. Ltd.

Library of Congress Cataloging-in-Publication Data

Karp, Gregory.
    Living rich by spending smart : how to get more of what you really want / Gregory Karp.
        p. cm.
    ISBN 0-13-235009-2 (pbk. : alk. paper) 1. Budgets, Personal. 2. Home economics—
Accounting. 3. Finance, Personal. I. Title.
    HG179.K374 2008
    332.024—dc22
                                                                        2007035095

For Dad and Grandpop,
role models and noble men

Contents

Acknowledgments

In 2003, Tribune Co. was creating a new personal finance section that would be available to all its newspapers, including the one where I worked, the *Allentown (PA) Morning Call*. That's when I successfully proposed a new kind of consumer column that I would write. We would call it "Spending Smart." It was first published in January 2004.

"Spending Smart" was an instant success with the millions of readers who buy Tribune Co. newspapers, which include the *Chicago Tribune*, *Baltimore Sun*, *Hartford Courant*, and *Orlando Sentinel*, among others. The column's success did not stem from my journalistic prowess. Rather, the topic of spending your money smarter struck a chord with readers. They had plenty of financial writers advising them on how to manage their extra money. But they didn't have someone telling them how to accumulate that money in the first place—how to spend their money smarter so they had some left over to manage. That's why they love the "Spending Smart" column.

Since the first column rolled off the presses, literally hundreds of readers have written and phoned with praise and criticism, both of which were invaluable. I am grateful and indebted to those readers.

"Spending Smart" the newspaper column—the genesis of the idea for this book—would never have achieved liftoff without initial and continuing support from several top-quality editors at the *Morning Call*. They are former Business Editor Michael Hirsch, Managing Editor David Erdman, and Editor Ardith Hilliard. I thank them for that.

This book also benefited from many of the experts I talked to along the way. They are far too numerous to mention by name, but I thank them nonetheless.

Thanks also to the folks at Pearson Prentice Hall, including Executive Editor Jim Boyd and Developmental Editor Russ Hall. Thanks too, to manuscript reviewers Liz Pulliam Weston, an author who also writes columns for *MSN Money*, and Cynthia Smith.

Thank you to Coach Deb, who helped me figure out what I wanted to do with my professional life. Those Sunday evening coaching sessions by phone led directly to this book. Thanks, sis.

Finally and most importantly, I want to thank my immediate family for unwavering support. There were too many times when Daddy couldn't pay enough attention to Jacob and Michael because he was cooped up in the home office tapping away at the computer keyboard at night, on weekends, and during holidays. And to my wife, Rebecca, thank you for your constant encouragement and boundless optimism. You are my inspiration.

About the Author

Gregory Karp is an award-winning, nationally published newspaper journalist. Greg's column, "Spending Smart," is consistently among the popular personal finance columns in Tribune Co. newspapers each Sunday. In 2006 the column was named Best Column by the Society of American Business Editors and Writers.

Greg's writing regularly appears in such newspapers as the *Chicago Tribune, Newsday, Baltimore Sun, Hartford Courant, Orlando Sentinel*, and *Allentown (PA) Morning Call*. It also appears on the Web sites of such television stations as WPIX in New York, WGN in Chicago, and KTLA in Los Angeles.

Greg often writes family money stories for *Better Homes and Gardens* magazine. He's a frequent guest on the morning show, *Good Day Philadelphia*, and appears weekly on RCN-TV in the Lehigh Valley, Pennsylvania. He maintains a blog at themorningcall.com.

Greg lives near Yardley, Pennsylvania, with his wife and two sons.

Introduction
The Spending Smart Philosophy

Controlling Spending Is the Key to Building Wealth

Spending Smart is the only way to get out of debt and build wealth. That's a bold, but true, statement. It's like calories are the key to a weight-loss diet. It doesn't matter what the new diet fad is. A diet to lose weight only works if you burn more calories than you consume. Everything else is just window dressing and hype.

In fact, controlling spending is far more important than the amount of your debt, which investments you choose, or even how much you earn. For people in debt, it wouldn't matter a bit if somebody graciously paid off all their credit cards or if they got a huge bonus at work to pay off the balances. Before long, they'd run up the card balance and be right back in serious debt because they didn't fix the fundamental problem, spending too much money. Americans today don't have a problem with debt. They have a problem with out-of-control spending. Debt is simply the result.

The truth is, you can't outearn dumb spending. Just ask all the multimillionaire Hollywood celebrities, sports stars, and lottery winners who ended up broke. Most people become wealthy and stay wealthy because they care as much about money going out as money coming in.

Spending Smart provides both the philosophy and the details to help you care about your spending too. If you already care, it will speed your trip to financial freedom and wealth.

The Truth About Getting Rich

The basic premise of wealth must be understood. It doesn't matter whether you earn $20,000 a year or $200,000. The only thing that makes you wealthier is regularly spending less money than you make.

That was proven in *The Millionaire Next Door*, a tremendous best-selling book that shattered myths about who America's millionaires really are. In fact, millionaires are not highly educated people who inherit a lot of money and spend it on obscene luxuries and pampered lifestyles.

Instead, they are hard-working people who, among other common attributes, care about what things cost and about getting good value for their money. In short, America's real millionaires—not those who just look the part—care about their spending. And you should too.

I like to think *The Millionaire Next Door* proved the philosophy, and this book provides the details.

Spending Smart is not about freeing up a few bucks here and there, but literally thousands of dollars, which compounded over a lifetime is the difference between struggling and being rich.

If getting rich isn't your goal, you still need to spend money smarter because money gives you options. You have options to quit a job and pursue a lifelong dream, options to give money to charitable causes that inspire you, and, in general, options to pursue what makes you happy.

Spending money smarter will help your relationships and maybe even your sex life. Without the desperation and fear that comes with money problems, all the relationships in your life can be more enjoyable.

You need to control spending to build wealth. It's the only way—outside an inheritance, lottery win, or some other windfall—you'll ever accumulate enough money to make it work for you. That means

getting money to start making its own money. For most people working normal jobs, there are not enough hours in a day to build wealth
simply from working for a wage or salary. Instead, you should spend
less and invest your money, whether in stocks, mutual funds, investment properties, your own business, whatever. All that matters is your
money is making money while you sleep.

For most people, it's the only way to get rich.

Learning to Spend Less

"Living below your means" is a simple and often-stated concept
in personal finance. But what isn't explained is how exactly to spend
money smarter, so you have some left over.

Many personal finance experts advise you to "pay yourself first,"
which is now a tired cliché for socking away money before you start
paying your bills. But that works only if have enough self-control not
to continue spending and simply throw the charges on a credit card.
That leads to the illogical situation many Americans face—saving
money in the bank at less than 5 percent interest at the same time
they're paying 18 percent interest on their credit cards. Their return
on that "investment" is negative 13 percent.

Ultimately, it all comes down to spending.

Standard cost-cutting advice makes sense, such as eating out at
restaurants less often and forgoing a fancy coffee every morning. But
it's not nearly enough to free up the thousands of dollars you need to
make a difference in your life.

What you need are both overall strategies and specific ways to
reduce spending. It's stuff you could probably research and figure out
for yourself, if only you had unlimited time and access to the nation's
leading experts. With those resources, you could investigate every
alternative to buying expensive ink-jet cartridges, figure out whether

extended warranties are a good deal, and read books on how to buy insurance.

But you don't have that time. So, you bought this book instead. With this book, you won't have to figure out for yourself which contradictory tips are true about saving money with home heating and cooling, for example. This book will just tell you. It will say, flat out, "This is right. This is wrong."

This book won't give you dozens of dopey ideas on saving a few pennies here and there—no tips on making your own laundry detergent or reusing dryer lint.

We'll cut to the chase and whack out the biggest offenders of wasteful spending and highlight the easiest cost cuts to make.

Spending Smart Is Not About Deprivation

Spending Smart is not a "live cheap, die loaded" plan or some exercise in fiscal anorexia.

Diets don't work if you're constantly hungry. And a plan to cut spending won't work if you have to say no to buying things you really want. The goal is to reallocate spending to satisfy all your needs and many of your wants.

You do that by plugging the leaks of wasteful spending and forcing your dollars to go where you want them to. It's about spending on purpose rather than by accident and habit.

Who cares which phone company is providing your dial tone? Switch to a lower-cost carrier and save hundreds of dollars per year. Insurance policies are generally the same. They guarantee a certain payout if bad things happen to you, a car accident, house fire, even death. Why would you pay more for one policy over another? And does a jar of sale-priced Skippy peanut butter taste any different than if you paid full price?

Life is full of spending choices, and making smarter decisions time after time adds up.

The average four-person household spends more than $62,000 a year, according to government statistics. Cutting spending by just 10 percent reaps a cool $6,200 a year, or $517 a month. That would go a long way toward paying off debt. Or, you could redirect that money into buying a nicer car or paying for a home improvement.

Or, if you started investing that money, you'd save more than $300,000 in cash in 20 years, assuming a modest 8 percent return.

That's the power of not spending.

Why Cutting Spending Works

In the short term, not spending a buck beats earning a buck every time. Here's why:

- Magnitude. You keep 100 cents of an unspent dollar but maybe 60 to 75 cents of an earned one, after taxes, Social Security, and the other deductions take their bite from your paycheck. Cutting out a $50-per-month cable TV bill is the same as a $30,000-a-year worker getting a year's pay raise of 3.3 percent, or $1,000. Benjamin Franklin said, "A penny saved is a penny earned." But that was before the era of income taxes. Today, a saved penny is worth far more than an earned one.

- Speed. Cutting spending is faster. You can cancel an expense, such as your gym membership, and start saving money today. You will be instantly better off. But it takes a long time to change your income. It may be months before you can get a pay raise at work, and overtime hours may be sporadically available. The only immediate thing you can do about income is to get a second job that starts this week. Or, as many Americans do, you can use fake income, such as a credit card that gives you an illusion that you have more cash. Of course, that just creates a crisis later when the credit card bill arrives.

- Control. You have more control over spending than income. You make dozens of spending decisions a day, from a morning mocha latte at Starbucks to whether you turn up the heat an extra degree in your home. However, your decisions about income are few on a daily basis, outside of resolving to get up and go to work so you aren't fired.
- Time well-spent. If you think you don't have time to reduce spending, convert the time you spend on cost-cutting to an hourly wage. A 2002 study at Virginia Tech University used students to comparison shop for various purchases. In one case, 16 minutes of comparing prices on the same model of color television saved $100. Converted to an hourly wage, that's $375 an hour. And if your total tax bite with Social Security amounts to 40 percent, it's the same as earning $625 an hour, or $1.3 million a year. Using the same math, spending three minutes clipping and using $10 worth of coupons pays $333 an hour. Taking 10 minutes to mail in a $50 rebate on a new computer printer earns you $500 an hour.

For those who enjoy sports metaphors, spending is like defense. Ask a knowledgeable fan of any major sport to identify the most important factor in winning, and you should get the same answer. "Offense is more exciting, with the home runs, the touchdown passes, the slam dunks," the fan will say. "But defense wins championships. It always has."

And so it is with money. Earning, the other major component to money, is more exciting and sexier, like offense. But for average people, winning with money ultimately depends on spending, your defense. It always has.

It's true that cutting costs is not a substitute for growing your income over the long term, but it allows you to get the most out of the income you have, whatever it is, today.

Spending Smart: A Proven Plan

Too many financial books are glad to tell you what to do with all your extra money, but how do you get that pile of cash in the first place? You spend your money smarter.

I know, because I've written more than 175 newspaper columns about spending money smarter. The columns appear in newspapers that together have millions of readers. Over the years, hundreds of readers have e-mailed and called to tell me how useful the tips were to them. Some gush about how easy it was to spend less money, all because they had the power of knowledge. Besides doling out advice in the newspaper column, I've also talked about Spending Smart on television, radio, and in my Web log, or blog.

I've interviewed the money gurus, from Suze Orman and David Bach to Dave Ramsey and Jean Chatzky. I've talked with Thomas J. Stanley, whose book *The Millionaire Next Door* changed our notions about the rich in America. And I've tapped the expertise of those who are not household names, but experts in their field, whether that's about manufacturer's coupons, emotional spending, or auto insurance.

And I've put these principles and tips into action in my own home, freeing up money to spend on things my family really cares about.

This book is organized into chapters with sections, each easily finished in a short sitting. Sections are essentially independent. You can read them in any order you like, with no plot or running theme to remember.

And don't be overwhelmed by the sheer volume of information and advice in this book. While it doesn't nearly cover all areas of spending in your life, it does provide literally hundreds of actionable tips. You don't need to implement all the Spending Smart advice right away, but you do need to get started today.

1

Financial FITness:
Whacking the Worst Offenders

The first steps in cutting spending painlessly can be summed up in a short acronym, FIT. It stands for food, insurance, and telecommunications. These are the three best categories in which to start your spending makeover. Reviewing these areas of spending will send you on your way to becoming financially FIT.

Why? Because you can reduce spending without depriving yourself, the savings are significant, and the typical waste is enormous.

Just as important, these are three areas of repeat spending. In other words, you'll be spending money in these areas again and again, every year for your whole life. For most people, that makes these expenses more costly than any one-time purchase, including a house.

The average family of four in America spends about $8,600 a year on food, $3,600 on insurance, and $1,300 on telecommunications, according to the U.S. Consumer Expenditure Survey. That's $13,500 a year in spending, or more than a quarter of all spending.

Then, figure you have to spend money in these areas for your entire adult life of, say, 50 years. That's $675,000 of lifetime spending, in today's dollars, on food, insurance, and telecommunications.

Granted, the proportion of spending in these areas might fluctuate during a lifetime. For example, food spending for retired empty-nesters might be less than for families with hungry teenagers. But the point is clear. These are areas of massive lifetime spending. And they're ripe areas for spending smarter.

Here's a prediction: After reading this chapter on food, insurance, and telecommunications, you will be able to save at least $1,000 this year, and probably much more. That means the first chapter alone will pay for the cover price of this book hundreds of times over and adequately compensate you for your time spent reading it.

Each FIT area has a mega-concept explained in more detail in following sections. These big-picture ideas alone can save significant money. They are:

- Food. Food spending has two main categories: eating in and eating out. The idea while grocery shopping is you generally shouldn't buy what you need. Instead, you should buy what's on sale and stockpile it. For eating out, the idea is to eat out on special occasions and because you want to, not because you're a poor meal planner.

- Insurance. The main idea here is you don't insure against little things. Insurance is to protect you from financial disaster, not nuisance expenses. And life insurance is to protect people who rely on your income no matter how you die. That usually means you just need plenty of term insurance, which is cheap.

- Telecommunications. This category refers to phone services. Make sure you're not paying for more service than you need. Telecom companies make pricing plans confusing on purpose, in hopes you'll overbuy. There's more competition than ever, so price and offerings change continually. Shopping for service beyond your traditional phone carrier is key.

Tackle these three areas, and you'll be financially FIT with little sacrifice.

Stockpiling Food for Savings: Bodega in the Basement

Weekly grocery shopping can be a major headache, but it's also a major source of painless spending cuts. One great strategy involves buying all the brand names you love and not clipping a single coupon.

It's stockpiling.

The first part of the strategy is keeping a price list, a simple notebook of prices on items you buy regularly. Then you'll know when something is truly on sale. You won't have to take the supermarket's word for it. For example, do you know whether $2.99 per pound is a good deal for boneless chuck steak? A quick look at your price list will answer that question.

The second part of the strategy is the key. You don't go shopping every week for what you need. Instead, you go to buy what's on sale that week. Then you load your pantry and freezer with sale-priced foods. When you run out of peanut butter, for example, you don't go to the store to buy it at full price; you fetch a jar from your own pantry that you bought on sale. Before long, if you're stockpiling in the basement, for example, you'll have a discount convenience store—or bodega—one floor down.

That's it—know what's on sale and buy only what's on sale. That's the stockpiling strategy.

Of course, exceptions to the stockpiling strategy include perishables, such as fresh fruits and vegetables and milk. And if you live in a small apartment with limited storage space for stockpiling food, the strategy will be less effective.

But for most people, stockpiling alone could save them 20 percent on the cost of food and nonfood items at the supermarket. Considering an American family of four spends a combined $6,700 a year on grocery-store food, housekeeping supplies, and personal-care items. Simply buying the exact same products but at sale prices would save $1,340.

Think about that: You go to the same supermarket you always went to, and you buy the exact same products, all brand names if that's what you prefer. The only difference is you buy them at the most favorable times. How easy is that?

Here are detailed tips to help with stockpiling:

- Get the flyers. Items on the front and back pages of the weekly supermarket circular are likely to have the deepest discounts. Supermarkets call them *loss leaders*, meaning the store actually sells the item so cheap it loses money. The idea is to entice you to visit the store and buy other items with high profit margins. Loss leaders are perfect stockpile items. If you missed the supermarket flyer for your favorite supermarket, go online to www.mygrocerydeals.com to look it up. And often flyers are available at the store.

- Play the cycle. Supermarket sales run in roughly 12-week cycles, so figure that items will go on sale about every three months. That means you don't have to go wild buying a year's worth of breakfast cereal because it will be on sale again fairly soon.

- Think nonfood items too. If you see a great sale on batteries, paper towels, or shampoo, stock up on those when they're on sale.

- Consider a second freezer. If you can get a secondhand food freezer that's fairly energy efficient, stockpiling frozen foods while they're on sale will more than pay for the freezer over time.

- Bring a calculator. Be sure to shop by unit price. For example, which is a better buy: four 12-packs of Coca-cola soft drink cans for $10 or a 6-pack of cans for $1.59? A calculator will help you figure the price per unit, which in this example is the price divided by the number of cans. The 12-packs are a better deal at less than 21 cents per can, while the 6-pack costs 26.5 cents per can. About a nickel per can doesn't sound like much savings until you figure your household might drink a case of soda a week. That's a savings of nearly $70 a year just for buying the exact same soda in 12-packs instead of 6-packs.

- Use warehouse clubs judiciously. Some staples, such as eggs and butter seldom go on sale at regular supermarkets. So, they might be cheaper at warehouse clubs, such as Sam's Club, Costco, and BJ's Wholesale, which sell many items in large quantities at a discount. However, warehouse clubs are hotbeds of temptation for buying items that are not such great deals. And you always have to be wary of buying perishable items in huge quantities because they might spoil before they're used, which will more than destroy your savings.

- Try store brands. People once derisively called them "generics." In recent years, store brands have improved immensely in quality. *Consumer Reports* magazine found that some are as good or better than name brands. In fact, the exact same manufacturers that make the comparable name-brand products make many store brands. At least try store brands for items you don't care much about—where average quality is acceptable. And try store-brand over-the-counter medications, such as aspirin. Formulations are regulated by the Food and Drug Administration and usually mirror the active ingredients found in name brands.

- Heed the usual advice. You've probably already heard such good tips as shop with a list to prevent impulse buys and not to shop hungry, which might prompt you to overbuy and stray from your stockpiling strategy. And remember to only buy convenience foods that significantly reduce hassle and are worth the cost. An obvious example is buying frozen orange juice concentrate instead of squeezing your own oranges.

Try stockpiling for three months to see whether it works for you. If it doesn't, you could always revert to buying groceries at full price. But most people will find they can save big money by not shopping for what they need, but shopping for what's on sale.

Coupon Clipping Conundrum: Hassle or Goldmine?

Shopper 1: "Clipping manufacturer coupons is a waste of my time—too much effort for too little savings."

Shopper 2: "Clipping coupons can save you hundreds of dollars a year because the little discounts really add up."

Who is correct? The answer is, they both are.

Coupons are a waste of time, *unless you use them correctly*. Clipping and filing little pieces of paper every time you see a coupon is a tremendous investment of time.

On the other hand, huge savings are available. Industrywide, manufacturers offered $331 billion in savings through coupons in 2006, according to CMS Inc., a coupon clearinghouse and operator of the coupon industry site CouponInfoNow.com.

An American family of four annually spends about $4,800 on grocery store food, as shown in Table 1.1.

TABLE 1.1   Food Spending in America

	Average	One Person	Family of Four
Food at home	$3,297	$1,638	$4,846
Food away from home	$2,634	$1,435	$3,776
Total food	$5,931	$3,073	$8,622

Source: Consumer Expenditure Survey, 2005

A four-person family also spends $800 on housekeeping supplies, $400 on personal-care products, and $130 on nonprescription drugs and vitamins, according to government figures on consumer expenditures. Those categories of items can be found at most supermarkets, and they all have coupons.

Super shoppers claim they save 50 percent, or half off, using a combination of sales and coupons. Their annual savings would be more than $3,000 for the average family of four.

So, what's the smart way to use coupons?

One of the basics of proper coupon use is to stockpile items when it's most advantageous to buy them, not when you need them. (See the previous section "Stockpiling Food for Savings" for details on the stockpiling strategy.) This eliminates the complaint, "They never have a coupon when I need it" because you always need it for your stockpile.

Here's how to use coupons for the biggest savings with the least hassle:

- Use the triumvirate of supermarket savings. Weekly sales, coupons, and supermarket loyalty cards are the three ways to get good deals on groceries. The goal is to use them together to get as much savings as possible. Avid coupon users regularly get items half off or even free.

- Don't clip. Instead of clipping Sunday newspaper coupons, save the whole glossy insert, from such companies as Smart-Source, Valassis, and Procter and Gamble. You don't even need to look at the coupons inside. Just write the date on the corner of the front page and file it in a drawer or container. When you're ready to go to the supermarket, go online to www.couponmom.com and search its free Newspaper Coupon Online Database for the item you're looking for. It will tell you the date of the glossy insert where you can find the coupon. For example, if you see a sale on the Gillette brand of razors you use, go to the online database to find the date a coupon was published for those razors. Then, pull the coupon circular to find a coupon to pair with the sale. Its Grocery Deals list helps you match a coupon with a store sale. A similar Web site called The Grocery Game at www.grocerygame.com also works well. That site charges a small fee of $5 a month but promises to tell you about unadvertised sales and clue you in when items hit "rock-bottom prices" at your supermarket.

- Look on Sundays. Newspaper coupons in the slick circulars on Sunday offer the biggest savings. Weekday coupons tend to have lower values, and you can skip them altogether if you don't have time to mess with them.

- Read the fine print. Look past the picture on the coupon and read the offer. Savings can apply to several sizes and varieties of related products other than just the one pictured.

- Smaller is better. When using a coupon, buying the smallest package that qualifies reaps the best savings. For example, $1 off a six-pack of soft drinks has a bigger percentage impact than $1 off a case.

- Double your savings. Using double-coupons savings, available at supermarkets in many parts of the country, is an obviously good idea, but it's not the only way to multiply savings. With two-for-one sales, also called "buy one get one free," you can often use two coupons because you're buying both items— even though you're getting one free.

- Shop on the best days. Go to the supermarket on Sunday, Monday, and Tuesday. Store sales generally start on Wednesdays, but the coupon to match that sale frequently doesn't come until Sunday. So, the time window to capitalize on both the sale and the coupon is best after you get the coupons on Sunday and before the next sale cycle begins on Wednesday.

- Use restraint. Coupons can prompt you to try new products and brands, and that's okay. But if you find coupons encourage you to buy more convenience foods and junk food, it won't be good for your wallet or your waistline. So, use coupons mostly to purchase items you already planned on buying.

- Print online coupons. You can print manufacturer coupons from many Web sites. These coupons tend to have higher dollar values than newspaper coupons, and you can print only the ones you want. Try such sites as SmartSource.com, Coupons.com, CoolSavings.com, and Eversave.com. Print the coupons in color and bring in the whole printed page, instead of cutting out coupons. The supermarket is more likely to accept it. Don't ever buy coupons from a Web site. They are likely to be fraudulent.

If you use coupons correctly, they can be more of a goldmine than a hassle.

Dining Out: Celebrations Versus Poor Meal Planning

Dining at restaurants once was reserved for special occasions, such as a birthday, wedding anniversary, or job promotion. But today, many families are eating out several nights a week, even when nobody really feels like it. Mostly, it stems from busy families not having enough time to prepare meals at home.

Meanwhile, making coffee at home for the commute or brown-bagging a lunch has become an almost quaint habit. In 1995, Americans spent less than 38 percent of their food budgets on eating out. Just a decade later, it was 44 percent, according to government figures on consumer expenditures. The rate is even higher among single people.

That trend is costing Americans, big-time.

A family of four spends about $3,800 a year on food away from home. That total isn't just celebratory dinners out, but vending-machine soft drinks, convenience-store snacks, McDonald's runs, delivered pizza, and take-out Chinese food.

What if you could cut in half your eating-out budget and still have all the special dinners out you wanted? You can. The secret is planning—planning to eat in and planning to take food and drink with you. Here's how:

- Freezer meals for dinner. Make weekday cooking easier by using freezer meals. When you're not rushed and have time to cook, make two or three times what you need for that night's dinner and freeze the rest. It doesn't take extra effort to make double or triple batches because the ingredients and cookware are out, and cleanup is about the same. So, instead of making a single meat loaf, make two or three. Triple the recipe for a casserole or make 20 hamburgers at a time. The payoff comes on a busy evening when you come home tired and maybe grumpy from work or running errands. Instead of falling back on eating out, you can grab one of your freezer meals and microwave it. It ends up being much cheaper and quicker than eating out, and usually winds up being more healthful too.

- Lunches. If you pay $6 each workday for lunch, whether at the company cafeteria or at a restaurant or deli, you're spending about $1,500 a year on lunches for one person. By contrast, bringing food and drink to work might cost about $2 a day, or $500. You must decide whether that $1,000-a-year difference is worth a few minutes to throw a lunch in a bag to bring to work. It could mean paying for a year of a child's education. How? If you instead invested that lunch money at 8 percent for a child's college education from birth to age 18, you would have about $40,000 on their high school graduation day, as shown in Table 1.2.

TABLE 1.2   Saving $4 a Day with a Brown-Bagged Lunch Turns into a Great Start Toward College Tuition

Child's Age	Growth on $1,000 Saved at 8% Return
1	$1,080
2	$2,246
3	$3,506
4	$4,867
5	$6,336
6	$7,923
7	$9,637
8	$11,488
9	$13,487
10	$15,645
11	$17,977
12	$20,495
13	$23,215
14	$26,152
15	$29,324
16	$32,750
17	$36,450
18	$40,446

Source: Calculated at dinkytown.net
Note: Final total could differ slightly depending on frequency of deposits.

- Day trips. Family excursions to the zoo, local swimming pool, amusement park, or even hiking and road trips, all can be done cheaper with planned-ahead food and drink. Even if you take convenience foods, such as prepackaged snacks, it will be cheaper than eating out.

- Beverages out. Celebratory dinners out might involve a beer or glass of wine. But try to skip the booze during more routine dining-out events. A glass of wine before you leave for the restaurant is one idea, assuming it won't impair your driving ability. Or plan to have a nightcap when you get home. Soft drinks out are wildly expensive for what you get. Try ordering free water with meals for a few restaurant outings and see whether you really miss your usual beverage.

- Keep the meal to one course. Surrounding a dinner with appetizers, coffee, and dessert is a lot of consumption at one sitting, especially considering today's large portion sizes. If the restaurant's desserts are special, plan to come back on a different night and just order coffee and dessert. Then you have two dining-out occasions for the price of one. A couple of light eaters could easily split an entree or order only appetizers.

- Dinner parties. Inviting friends over for a home-cooked meal accomplishes the same social interaction and enjoyment as going out to dinner but without the restaurant prices. Swapping dinner parties with friends, neighbors, and relatives could also cut down on the need for baby-sitters if you can bring the kids along.

- Coupons. Many nicer restaurants, not just the chains, offer coupons with significant values. One place to look online is Restaurant.com, which sells dining certificates. A typical offer is a $25 certificate for $10. Others are DinnerBroker.com for off-peak dining, and OpenTable.com has a rewards points system. I cashed in on a super deal at Restaurant.com when it offered a special coupon code for 70 percent off. So I bought a $25 coupon to one of the nicest restaurants in my area and paid just $3, clearing $22 for a few minutes on the computer. Many metropolitan areas have Entertainment Books full of dining coupons. See details at www.entertainment.com or get them even cheaper through an AAA or other membership. Also, look for Entertainment Books in midsummer, when they're sold at a deep discount. Just be aware that you'll only get a few months worth of value—instead of a year—before coupons expire.

Turn back the clock and make dining out a special event again. Your bank account will thank you.

Life Insurance: It's Your Money and Your Life

Shopping around for better prices on life insurance has always been a good idea, but plummeting prices over the past decade have made it imperative for spending smart.

If you haven't looked at rates for term life insurance recently, you're probably wasting big money. It's like continuing to pay 1998 prices for a DVD player that today costs just $50.

Life insurance premiums are less than half what they were in the mid-1990s, as shown in Table 1.3. Today, a 40-year-old nonsmoking man rated in standard health pays $685 a year *less* than a similar man in 1994; that's nearly $7,000 difference over a decade.

TABLE 1.3   Premiums for $500,000 of Term Life Insurance, 40-Year-Old Male Nonsmoker

Year	Preferred Rating	Standard Rating
1994	$995	$1,300
1995	$830	$1,050
1996	$660	$960
1997	$583	$954
1998	$515	$695
1999	$425	$670
2000	$480	$690
2001	$420	$740
2002	$395	$745
2003	$375	$725

Year	Preferred Rating	Standard Rating
2004	$375	$715
2005	$375	$660
2006	$352	$641
2007	$340	$615

Source: Insurance Information Institute

And it's not that big a hassle to switch policies. A couple hours of work can save literally hundreds of dollars per year.

So, you should "refinance" your life insurance. It's similar to refinancing your home mortgage to get a better interest rate, trading a higher house payment for a lower one. With insurance, you can get the same policy for less money. Or you can buy a policy with a bigger payout without increasing your premiums. And the beauty of refinancing your life insurance is that there are no closing costs like there are with refinancing a mortgage. The insurance company pays for the switching costs, such as the medical exam and paperwork. You begin saving right away.

Contemplating the financial fallout from your death is no fun, but it's part of being a grown-up when other people depend on your income. Here are some straightforward questions and answers about life insurance and "refinancing" your policy to save money:

- What is it exactly? Life insurance should be relatively simple. The insurance company pays your beneficiaries an agreed amount of money if you die. For example, if a middle-aged man with a $500,000 policy dies, his beneficiary, usually his wife, would get half a million dollars. She'll use the money to pay for regular living expenses, kids' college, building a retirement fund, and other costs of life. It replaces the income the man would have earned if he had lived. However, life insurance becomes complicated if you buy anything but term insurance. The alternative, cash value insurance, has an investment component tied to the life insurance. Cash-value insurance has many built-in fees and a lousy rate of return on the investment portion. So, most people don't need to consider anything but term insurance. And term is so much simpler. If you want to invest, that's great. Just do it separately from insurance.

- Who needs it? Breadwinners who have other people such as a spouse and/or children depending on their income need life insurance. The top earner in the family would be an obvious choice. And you might even need a small policy on a stay-at-home mom, for example. The surviving husband might have to pay for services the mom provided, such as child daycare, after-school care, or possibly domestic help for household chores such as cooking and cleaning. The bottom line on buying life insurance for yourself is to ask, "Would anybody be financially distressed if I died?"

- Who doesn't need it? Children don't need life insurance. Almost nobody depends on a child's income to survive, and statistically very few children die. If your family would face financial ruin from paying for a child's funeral and burial expenses, a small term policy might be appropriate. Otherwise, skip child life insurance. Other types of people who don't need life insurance are childless single people, independently wealthy people, and retirees with substantial nest eggs to last them their lifetime.

- How much do I need? You have to decide how much life insurance you need and for how long. Consider such factors as your income, mortgage balance, and college expenses for kids. A general rule of thumb is six to ten times your gross annual income. If college expenses are your main concern, get a term policy to cover you at least through graduation of the last student. Other people might want coverage to last until your expected retirement date. Because term insurance is relatively inexpensive, err on the high side, especially because inflation will eat away at the value of the payout as time goes by. The Internet has dozens of online calculators to help you specifically assess your needs for life insurance. Use your favorite search engine to find "life insurance needs calculator." However, with those assessment tools you might find you're doing a lot of guessing about your future needs for money, rates of investment return, and inflation. You might be better off just buying insurance equal to six to ten times your income.

- How do I compare policies? Your first stop would be with your current life insurer. Ask about current rates. Then you could call other insurers for quotes, but that can be time consuming. It's more efficient to go online and use insurance comparison services. Good ones include AccuQuote.com, Term4Sale.com, InsWeb.com, and Insure.com. Use more than one comparison tool. It seems each has affiliations with different insurers. Don't assume buying extra life insurance through your employer is the best deal, especially because you'll likely lose the insurance if you switch jobs.

- How do I switch policies? It is critical to do things in the correct order. Activate your new life insurance policy before canceling the old one. Nobody knows for sure whether they'll flunk a medical exam for a new policy—if a previously undiscovered disease or ailment is found, for example. The new condition might preclude you from qualifying for life insurance from any company. That's why you need to keep your current policy in effect until a new one is active. If the worst is discovered, at least you'll have your old policy.

- Is the insurer I chose safe? Term policies are mostly the same, so the brand of insurance company you choose doesn't matter much, as long as it's highly rated. After you choose a company, look up its rating at such free Web sites as A.M. Best, www.ambest.com, or Standard & Poor's, www.standardandpoors.com. Reports are free with free registration. Highly rated companies should all pay the life insurance claim and pay it in a timely manner.

- What if I already have a cash-value policy? Cash-value "permanent" policies come in different flavors, generally called *whole*, *universal*, and *variable life insurance*. There are many good reasons to cash out or "surrender" your cash-value policy, replacing it with a term life insurance policy. For one, term insurance will be far cheaper—in some cases nearly ten times cheaper—meaning you can either save or invest the difference or get a lot more term coverage for the same money. Although you may incur financial penalties to get out of a cash-value policy, it could be worth it. For $75 or less, the Consumer Federation of America will evaluate your cash-value policy and make recommendations. Visit www.consumerfed.org or call 603-224-2805.

The short version on refinancing your life insurance is this: Shop for a good price on term insurance from a reputable company. Sign the papers and take the medical exam. Cancel your old policy. Put the saved money toward something you really care about.

Home and Auto Insurance: Don't Pay Too Much

Auto accidents, house fires, theft, and similar unpleasant events are no fun to think about. And after you have these insurance coverages in place, it's easy to think you're done. But revisiting your home and auto insurances regularly can pay off handsomely in saved money. And, in fact, your need for coverage changes over time.

The average family spends $847 a year on auto insurance and $776 on home insurance. Ultimately, insurance is just a cold, unemotional contract. You pay premiums to an insurance company, and it pays you if a financially devastating event happens. So, as long as the company is reputable and highly rated, it doesn't matter which one you choose. You can shop by price.

Two main tasks can save big money on auto and home insurance:

- Compare premiums. Premiums for both auto and home insurance can vary widely among companies, so it pays to comparison shop. Get at least three price quotes, and make sure you're comparing the exact same coverage. You can call companies directly or compare premiums on Internet sites, such as www.insurance.com, www.instantquote.com, or www.insweb.com. Your state insurance department may also provide comparisons of prices charged by major insurers. Don't become emotionally attached to any single insurance company. And forget about paying higher premiums because you think you'll get better service. A 2005 study by the Consumer Federation of America found no correlation between price and service. Your insurance company might drop you after just a few speeding tickets or car accidents, so this is no time to be company-loyal. But make sure the company is reputable. Check with your state insurance department and a database at www.naic.org/cis. Also check rating agency Web sites, such as www.ambest.com and www.standardandpoors.com.

- Raise deductibles. A *deductible* is the amount of money you have to pay before your insurance kicks in. A $200 auto insurance deductible means that if you're in an auto accident that causes $1,000 of damage to your car, the insurance company pays you just $800. That's because you're responsible for the first $200. Nobody wants to pay more out-of-pocket than they have to, but you're handsomely rewarded for taking that risk. Higher deductibles on your car alone could yield savings of 15 to 30 percent or more, says the Insurance Information Institute. So, that could mean more than $250 savings a year. So raise your auto deductibles to at least $500 or $1,000 if you can. You might opt for an even higher deductible on homeowners insurance. For example, raising your home insurance deductible from $250 to $5,000 could save 37 percent on premiums. Meanwhile, stash away several hundred dollars to cover higher deductibles if you have a claim.

The main idea with all insurance is that you buy it to protect yourself from financial disaster, not annoyances, inconveniences, or financial pinches. That same concept applies to deductibles. Get a high enough deductible that you can save significant money, even though you might feel the bite of paying it. But set it lower than an amount that would spell extreme hardship or financial ruin. If you have a super-low $100 deductible on auto or homeowners insurance, call your agent today and raise it.

Here are a few other ways to save on insurance:

- Get discounts. Make sure you're getting all the policy discounts you're entitled to. Auto insurance discounts may apply for low mileage, belonging to AAA, antitheft devices, driver-training courses, and car-safety features, such as antilock brakes or airbags. A teen driver with good grades often gets a discount.

And, of course, you pay less if you've demonstrated you're a safe driver. Deadbolt locks, burglar alarms, and smoke detectors can lower rates for home insurance. Also ask about a multipolicy discount for having home and auto coverage with the same company. That price break alone can run 5% to 15%. Teens might get a break on auto insurance if they leave a car home while they're in college, and retirees might get a discount on homeowners insurance because they're home all day, which lessens the chances of burglary and fire.

- Reduce coverage on old cars. Consider dropping collision and comprehensive coverage on older cars. It may not be cost-effective to continue to buy this coverage on cars worth less than ten times the amount you would pay for the coverage. For example, the break-point for a $3,000 car is $300 in nonliability coverage. Usually, you're a candidate to drop coverage if your car is worth less than about $2,500. Find out what your car is worth at the Kelly Blue Book Web site, www.kbb.com.

- Maintain good credit. Insurers are increasingly using credit-based insurance scores to set auto coverage premiums. That's because studies show that people with good credit tend to file fewer claims. Check your credit report free at www.annual-creditreport.com. You'll have to pay for a three-digit credit score at the previously mentioned site or www.myfico.com.

- Cut waste. Don't double-pay for coverage. For example, if you have a vehicle-towing plan through AAA, make sure you're not paying for it on your auto insurance policy. Say no to optional insurance at the car-rental counter if your auto policy already covers rentals. Review your policies regularly to make sure they still reflect your current life. For example, you could lower your coverage if your teen driver went away to college, if your work commute shortened considerably, or if you sold a valuable collectible that doesn't need personal property coverage anymore. For home insurance, remember to insure just the value of the house, not the land it sits on. For more information, see a helpful Web site developed by the National Association of Insurance Commissioners at www.insureuonline.org.

When bad things happen, you want to have the right insurance to protect yourself from financial disaster, but you don't want to overpay.

Phone at Home: Pay Less for Your Landline

Getting your spending right on your home phone service isn't difficult, but you must regularly match what you use compared with what's offered in the fast-changing telecommunications marketplace. The good news is you can almost certainly cut your telecom spending if you know a few basic strategies.

American households that use landline local and long-distance phone services spend an average of $50 a month, or $600 a year, according to market-research firm TNS Telecoms.

The basic concept behind not overpaying for home phone service is to avoid wasting money by paying for services you don't use or over-buying on services that you do use. Here's how to avoid that:

- Choose a long-distance plan. Whatever you do, don't remain on the phone company's default long-distance plan. It's the most expensive way to make out-of-town calls. First, call your current long-distance carrier and ask what plan is right for your calling patterns. Or go to its Web site for information on plan choices. Then compare those plans to other long-distance offerings. Call quality is mostly the same no matter which long-distance company you choose, so it makes sense to shop by price. You should be able to tailor your long-distance service to fit your calling habits. That's easiest to do at such Web sites as ABTolls.com, TRAC.org, MyRatePlan.com, WhiteFence.com, PhoneRateFinder.com, CheapTelephoneBills.com, and Save-OnPhone.com.

- Beware the bundle. Bundles of services are wildly popular among phone and cable companies. But the industry secret is that these "money-saving" bundles, which often include unlimited long-distance service, are likely to cost you more money than if you bought services a la carte from different providers. Although paying one bill each month is more convenient, it's worth comparing prices to determine just how much extra you're paying for that simplicity. For example, if you pay $13 a month for unlimited interstate long-distance service and only make an hour's worth of long-distance calls, you're paying about 22 cents per minute. Meanwhile, the best rates for long-distance service are less than a nickel a minute, including fees, for one hour of talking. So, the unlimited plan is quadruple the price or more than $10 a month extra in this example. Put another way, the bundle doesn't beat the best a la carte long-distance plans until you make about eight hours of long-distance calls every month. As a more general rule, if you make less than five hours a month of long-distance calls, skip the bundle. Instead, go to the comparison Web sites mentioned previously and seek a low-cost long-distance provider.

- Use wireless only. Many more people today are reducing land-line costs by canceling it. Instead, they use a mobile phone for all local and long-distance calls. This isn't a strategy for every-one, but it's especially good for single people who aren't home often. And it avoids hassles of divvying up the phone bill with roommates. Obviously, it's not a good idea for people who use their telephone line for Internet access or home security sys-tems. And make sure you have good wireless phone reception in your home before you cut the cord. A less radical plan is to cancel your long-distance service only and use the mobile phone for long-distance calls, which most plans include for no additional charge. Make sure you have enough "anytime" min-utes to avoid expensive per-minute charges.

- Consider VoIP. Voice over Internet Protocol, pronounced "voyp," sounds techie, but it's becoming a mainstream way to use your high-speed Internet service as your phone line. With paid services, such as market-leader Vonage, you can use a nor-mal telephone and keep your same phone number. Installation involves attaching a small box to your high-speed Internet con-nection and plugging a regular phone into the box. VoIP kits can be found at many big-name electronics stores. Such com-panies as Vonage, Packet8, and even traditional phone carriers offer unlimited local and long-distance VoIP calling packages at nearly half the price of similar traditional landline packages, with fewer junk fees and taxes. And they tend to offer a ton of calling features, far beyond call waiting and caller ID, for no additional cost. Call quality is generally good with VoIP, without echoes or delays, but will only be as good as your broadband connection. And realize your phone service won't work during outages in your electricity or Internet service. For that reason, it's good to have a wireless phone too, perhaps with a car charger or backup battery.

• Try free Internet calls. Other services that use VoIP are free and don't use phone numbers. Instead, they use a small software program on your Internet-connected computer to talk to anyone else in the world with the same software on their computer. The disadvantage is you are tethered to your computer with a microphone and speakers, or a headset that includes both. If you want to try VoIP before committing to a paid plan, try a free service first. The most popular choice is Skype, www.skype.com, which is owned by online auction site eBay. Similar offerings come from instant messenger services such as Windows Live Messenger, Google Talk, AOL's AIM Triton, Yahoo! Messenger with Voice, and ICQ. Besides free calls, Skype and most of the IM services also offer paid services for calling real phone numbers—landline or wireless—from your computer or receiving calls on your computer from conventional phones. Internet calling, even if you have to pay a modest fee, becomes well worth the hassle if you make many expensive international calls.

• Dial extra digits. Prepaid phone cards and dial-around numbers are another way to lower your long-distance bill. Both require you to dial a few extra digits on your home phone. You can buy prepaid cards at such wholesale clubs as BJ's, Sam's Club, and Costco. The rates are usually rock-bottom, many less than 5 cents a minute. When making a call, you usually enter an access code and then the phone number you want to call. Most modern phones allow you to program such an access code into your telephone so you don't have to hunt for the card each time you call. A warning, though: Stick with cards from reputable retailers and long-distance carriers. With dial-arounds, you dial 10-10 plus a three-digit prefix before the number you want to call. A comparison of dial-arounds is available online at www.10-10PhoneRates.com. Watch the fine print for connect fees, monthly minimums, and other gotchas.

- Skip the add-ons. Even if you don't change the way you make calls, you can save money by examining your add-on services, such as call waiting, caller ID, three-way calling, call forwarding, and voicemail. They can cost several dollars apiece. The dirty little secret of the telephone industry is that most of those services cost very little to provide, but then they charge you $8 a month for caller ID and $3 for call waiting. Wire insurance, often called "wire maintenance" is optional. Most people can cancel the several-dollar monthly charge, which is a kind of insurance for problems with inside phone wiring and jacks. If you have wire maintenance, wiring repair inside your house is free. However, those repairs are rare, unless you have a very old house.

- Dial smart. Directory assistance is an expensive service for what you get, often costing $1 or more per look-up if you use 411 or the older 555-1212. Phonebooks and Internet look-up sites are free. Sites include www.switchboard.com, www.smartpages.com, www.superpages.com, and www.infospace.com. It also helps to maintain a good list of regularly called numbers. A free service called 1-800-FREE411, which is the number you dial to use it, will look up a number for free, but you have to listen to a ten-second advertisement. If you're looking for a toll-free number, dial 800-555-1212 to get a free look-up.

The last thing to know about home phone service is that offerings change frequently, and it can pay to keep on top of the latest telecom choices. For example, I got a brochure in my phone company bill that outlined a calling bundle similar to the one I already had—for my needs, it turned out a bundle was, in fact, a good way to go.

The lower-tier bundle was similar to the one I had but didn't include free calls to Canada, which I rarely used; three-way calling, which I never used; and speed-dialing, which I never bothered learning how to use. So, I dropped down to the cheaper plan and saved $15 a month. That was possible only because I knew the cheaper plan existed. Reading about the plan online and calling the phone company to switch plans took about ten minutes. That's $180 a year in savings, just because I bothered to read an advertisement that came with my phone bill. In fact, it's not unusual for me to change phone plans several times a year, as better deals become available. Chances are, you could save money too.

Wireless Mobile Phone: Don't Let Them Cell You a Bad Plan

Americans today spend far more on their wireless phone service than their home phone service.

Households that pay for wireless phone service spend an average of about $84 a month, according to TNS Telecoms as shown in Table 1.4. That's 66 percent more than households spend on a landline phone.

TABLE 1.4 Household Spending on Phone Services

Service	Average Monthly Expenditure
Local	$37.31
Long distance	$13.60
Wireless	$84.41

Source: TNS Telecoms, 2007

The most basic advice is to shop the phone plan instead of the phone handset. You'll ultimately be satisfied or dissatisfied by the service rather than the device. Even if you pay $200 or $300 for a fancy handset, you'll pay far more than that on service during your first six months.

Here are other ways to cut wireless spending:

- Ditch it. Think critically about the convenience of having a wireless phone versus the cost. Fifteen years ago, people seemed to get along well without one. Having a cell phone plan "for an emergency" is mostly a lame excuse. Just about any charged cell phone can dial 911 with no service plan at all.

A friend or relative would be glad to give you an older cell phone that she has stashed in a drawer. Canceling service may require you to pay an early termination fee, but it may be worth it. For example, paying $175 to cancel service seems like a lot, but it's cheaper than continuing to pay $50 or $80 a month for another 18 months, which amounts to $900 to $1,440. Another option for getting out of your plan is to transfer the contract to someone else. Until recently, that meant you had to find friends or family members interested in assuming the contract. But now, an online service can match wireless customers who want to dump a contract with ones who want one. One swap service is found online at www.celltradeUSA.com. The benefit for the buyer is avoiding activation fees in most cases, being responsible for only the balance of the contract, and possibly receiving a negotiated cash incentive from the seller. Be aware that the company charges the seller about $20 for making the match. You also should check the transfer details in your own contract and be careful how you complete the transfer if you want to preserve the same phone number with a different wireless provider. Including a wireless phone in the deal is optional.

- Right-size. Compare how many minutes per month you actually use to the number of minutes in your plan. Are you paying for more minutes than you need? Most people are. It might be a good idea to downgrade your plan to include fewer minutes, even if you have to pay extra on occasion for exceeding your allotted minutes. It could be cheaper than paying $10 or $20 more every month for a bigger bucket of minutes. To help determine your ideal number of minutes, use a rule of thumb provided by the nonprofit Telecommunications Research & Action Center: If you regularly use 200 minutes fewer than your monthly allotment, drop down a tier of service. If you consistently exceed your allotment by 100 minutes, consider going up a tier.

- Skip the extras. Lighten up on the text messaging, extra ringtones, and cell-phone video games, all of which cost extra. If your teen must have text messaging, which is basically like sending short e-mails from phone to phone, examine your provider's price packages. Make sure the package fits your actual texting use. When you are near a computer, send text messages from the PC to a friend's phone, which is free. And consider whether you really need Internet access on your cell phone. Is it really useful or just a toy you haven't used since the novelty wore off?

- Coordinate plans. If you regularly talk on the phone to the same friends and family members, try to get everybody on the same network. Using plentiful in-network minutes instead of valuable anytime-any network minutes may allow you to drop down a tier of service and pay less.

- Prepay. You are not stuck signing a cell-phone contract. Pay-as-you-go prepaid wireless plans continue to improve, as providers offer cheaper phones and lower rates. Traditional post-paid wireless service remains cheaper per minute, but that assumes you use all the minutes. Post-paid rapidly becomes more expensive if you have dozens or even hundreds of unused minutes every month. Another advantage is that prepaid minutes already include the fees, surcharges, and taxes that show up as separate line items on your wireless bill and add 20% to 30% to the bottom line. That further closes the per-minute price gap between prepaid and post-paid. For lighter users of mobile phones—those who use less than 200 or even 300 minutes per month—prepaid service may well be the less expensive choice. Check out the company Tracfone and such usual carriers at T-Mobile and Verizon. Beware that prepaid minutes can expire in as few as 30 days. Leftover minutes—and the money that purchased them—are wasted, just as minutes in most traditional plans are wiped out and renewed each month. Typically, the more minutes you buy with prepaids, the longer the minutes live.

- Accessorize online. Shop for car chargers, hands-free sets, leather cases, and extra batteries at online stores or auction sites, such as eBay. Prices are much lower than at wireless retail stores. Be aware that some of the accessories may not be from the original manufacturer and may be lower quality, but most cheap car-chargers, for example, do the job well.

- Get your company to pay for it. If you often use your personal wireless phone for business calls, make a case to your boss for getting a company cell phone. Or try to arrange some type of reimbursement plan for business calls made on your personal phone.

- Shop around. Compare your plan with competitors and consider switching. You can now keep the same phone number when you switch. But while you could save upwards of $20 a month for similar plans, don't compare on price alone. A service plan is virtually worthless if the new provider has spotty coverage in your area and you're constantly dropping calls or getting no signal. Use the carrier's free trial period to determine whether service works where you need it.

- Ringtones. If you change ringtones frequently, it could get expensive. It costs more to download a 20-second ringtone from a song, often $2 or $3, than it does to download the entire song, often 99 cents. But you can make your own ringtone for free by using software to create an audio clip from a song on your computer and transferring it to your phone, assuming it supports MP3 ringtones. You transfer the file by USB cord, via Bluetooth wireless connection, or as an e-mail or text-message attachment. Many tutorials on the Internet explain how to do this. Many Web sites, such as mobile17.com, facilitate the process for free, and paid software can make it easier too. While do-it-yourself ringtones are much cheaper, realize that if you want just a few new tones, paying for them is a lot less hassle.

2

Know Thine Enemy; It Is Us:
The Problem Between Our Ears

If it's true that knowledge is power, then understanding why we're not already spending money brilliantly can be an epiphany. Once revealed, it can be the "ah-hah" moment that changes everything.

The problem is, many people don't take time to examine where their money is going and make a conscious decision about whether it's going to worthwhile use.

Are you spending your money on purpose, or by accident and habit?

Ultimately, your current financial situation is the sum result of the many money decisions you make every day of your life. If you make more good decisions than bad, you'll be financially comfortable. Too many bad decisions, and you struggle.

Many of us know and have been inspired by the final lines in a Robert Frost poem:

Two roads diverged in a wood

And I took the one less traveled by

And that has made all the difference

Every day, we're confronted with spending decisions that represent fork after fork in the road. Sometimes it's a decision to spend or not to spend. Other times, it's to spend on item A or item B. Still other times, it's to spend now or spend later.

Repeatedly making good decisions puts you on the road to prosperity. But make no mistake, to spend smarter, you certainly will have to make some decisions other people—broke people—wouldn't. In other words, you'll have to take the road less traveled. And I guarantee you, it will make all the difference.

The truth is, dumb spending doesn't stem from lack of knowledge—not knowing you could get a better price on a box of tissues or tires for your car. It's born of consumer behavior. These behaviors are repeated over and over again in every spending decision—at every fork in the road.

Smart People, Dumb Spending: Fire the Accountant in Your Head

Imagine you're in a downtown store, considering buying a fabulous pair of shoes for $75. Another customer notices. "Hey, I just saw that same shoes on sale at Bloomingdale's for $50," she says. It's a five-block walk.

This is a spending decision that represents a fork in the road. Do you walk the five blocks for the better deal? Most people would say yes, research shows.

Now imagine you're eyeing a $2,500 living room set and learn the same set is available five blocks away for $2,475. Do you hoof it to the other store?

Surprisingly, most people would not. Now, think about that. The underlying question is exactly the same: "Is it worth walking five blocks to save $25?"

It doesn't matter whether you answered yes or no. It only matters that you realize the decision should be the same in either scenario. But smart people make irrational decisions almost daily.

In the preceding example, which illustrates what experts call *mental accounting*, a dollar doesn't always equal a dollar. In the context of a $75 pair of shoes, the $25 was significant. Some people immediately see it as a huge 33 percent savings. In a purchase of $2,500, it seems miniscule, just 1 percent.

But our pocketbooks and bank accounts don't know the percentages. They just know the decision is about $25.

That's why people think nothing of saying yes to extras while buying a car, for example. Floor mats that cost $200 seem inexpensive compared with the cost of a new $25,000 car. But if you went into an auto parts store the next day and saw floor mats being sold for $200, they would seem laughably overpriced.

Mental accounting is why it's so easy to lose back $500 in casino gambling winnings and not care. In our minds, those won dollars don't hold the same value as dollars earned on the job. Yet, obviously, the value is the same.

Here are other ways our irrational selves get us into money trouble, according to consumer-behavior research:

- Loss aversion. Most people are inordinately afraid of losing money. They feel much more pain from a loss than joy from a gain. That's why people hold on to bad investments, hoping to get even before they sell. Even if they know the investment is unlikely to rise in value, they hold onto it for fear of making a paper loss a real one. That behavior begs the logical question, "Why keep money in a bad investment hoping to get even, when you can move money to a good investment to try to get even?" It's because of the pain we feel from loss.

- Sunk costs. The so-called *sunk cost fallacy* is why people will venture out in a dangerous snowstorm to attend a concert because they paid $100 for tickets. But if they had free tickets, they would skip it and stay home. You won't get money back in either case. It's also why you might spend more money on car repairs because you've spent so much on repairs already or finish reading a bad book because you've invested several hours to get halfway through. The point is to leave the past behind and make money decisions based on the present and future.

- Endowment effect. Often we place a higher value on what we already have, compared with what we could have. Examples are remaining in a low-paying job because it's comfortable, keeping retirement money in ultra-safe investments because of confusion on choices, or failing to return an inferior product with a warranty. That's why marketers use trial periods and money-back guarantees. They know that people are very unlikely to return the product after they take possession of it.

- Innumeracy. Math illiteracy or ignorance about numbers can be costly. It's why we think a 3 percent pay raise is okay during a time of 4 percent inflation. In fact, you're actually poorer because your money lost purchasing power. If people who gambled on state lotteries truly understood the odds of winning, they would never buy a lottery ticket again. It's why people have low insurance deductibles, when the probability of filing a claim dictates they should pay lower premiums for higher deductibles. And it's why young people don't appreciate the near-magical power of compounding investment returns. Take Table 2.1, for example, which shows the power of compounding by doubling a penny every day for a month.

TABLE 2.1   Would You Rather Have $1 Million or the Final Amount of a Penny Doubled Every Day for a Month?

Day of the Month	Penny Doubled
1	$0.01
2	$0.02
3	$0.04
4	$0.08
5	$0.16
6	$0.32
7	$0.64
8	$1.28

Day of the Month	Penny Doubled
9	$2.56
10	$5.12
11	$10.24
12	$20.48
13	$40.96
14	$81.92
15	$163.84
16	$327.68
17	$655.36
18	$1,310.72
19	$2,621.44
20	$5,242.88
21	$10,485.76
22	$20,971.52
23	$41,943.04
24	$83,886.08
25	$167,772.16
26	$335,544.32
27	$671,088.64
28	$1,342,177.28
29	$2,684,354.56
30	$5,368,709.12

- Anchors away. How much should a man spend on a diamond engagement ring? Of course, the answer is only as much as he can afford. But because the diamond industry tells us the anchor value should be two months' salary, every judgment he makes about the ring's price is likely to be measured against that recommendation. Likewise, some investors may judge a stock's price against its unwarranted all-time high, which becomes the anchor, instead of a price based on more relevant measures of company performance.

- Ego. With money decisions, overconfidence may lead you to make poor purchasing decisions because you think you know more than you do about a product or brand. Or you may try to sell your house by yourself to save a sales commission but end up with a far lower sales price. Ego is why investors think they can pick a mutual fund that will beat the market average when, over time, two-thirds to three-quarters of all mutual funds fail to do that.

The point of highlighting these consumer failures is the hope that once exposed, they might provide you an "ah-hah" moment and put you on a path to smarter spending.

Evaluating Value: Psychological Income

Save money by spending on what you care about.

That short sentence encompasses a philosophy that will help you not only spend less but also get more satisfaction from the money you spend.

You do that by training yourself to measure your own *psychological income*, or the nonfunctional benefit from a purchase, especially a name-brand purchase. It represents how the product or service makes you feel.

On the surface, that concept might seem hokey. But it pervades the American consumer's life and is well-established in the world of marketing. Often the term psychological income refers to supplementing job income. For example, a social worker's income is paid in dollars, plus the satisfaction of helping people.

But psychological income applies to spending, too. It's probably most obvious in car buying. All reasonably reliable automobiles will get you from home to work, for example. That's the functional component of the buying decision. Some will get you to work in more comfort, with a smoother ride, superior handling, an upgraded audio system, and better heating and air conditioning. Those are real benefits that apply to everyone buying that vehicle.

But you might derive yet another benefit, a psychological one, that comes from driving a BMW, Mercedes, Lexus, or other high-end vehicle. It could make you feel a sense of accomplishment because you have reached a level of wealth to afford it. Or it might make you feel better about yourself, even superior to other drivers. Buying a Jeep might make you feel adventurous. Buying a Volvo might make you feel safe. Buying a hybrid gas-electric car might make you feel like an environmentalist.

Other car buyers don't get a psychological benefit from a car purchase. They just want a vehicle to get them to and from work. It would be a total waste of money for them to buy a luxury car.

So psychological income is highly individual. Reading product reviews and evaluations, such as those in *Consumer Reports*, can help you judge quality and value. But they cannot measure for you the satisfaction you derive from the purchase.

For example, a man might care a great deal about his brand of golf clubs and get satisfaction from them during every round of golf. But he couldn't care less about the tools and appliances in his kitchen. Meanwhile, a woman who loves cooking gourmet meals gets great satisfaction from having a top-quality set of kitchen knives and a nice-looking stainless steel high-end stove. But she doesn't care about the brand of golf clubs she uses on weekends. Those two people should spend different amounts on their golf clubs and kitchen appliances.

Consumers with a limited income—which includes most everybody—have to make trade-off decisions and can't afford to buy top quality for every purchase.

The point is to spend more when you care more. If you don't care so much, choose functional brands. It can save real money and lead to more satisfaction because your money is going toward expenses you care most about. It might even make shopping easier, considering the plethora of choices available for most purchases. In other words, it helps you purchase on purpose.

Money not spent on a brand name could go to savings for future purchases or other immediate purchases that matter more to you.

How do you decide whether to pony up more money for an elite brand? Measure the PI—psychological income—for purchases in your life. Here's how:

- Make a list. Write down the major categories of spending in your life. If you're already maintaining a household budget, this part should be easy.

- Evaluate PI. In a column next to those spending categories, write 1 for the lowest level of psychological income you derive from the purchase. Place a 2 beside those that provide a moderate level of emotional satisfaction, and write a 3 next to those that dramatically affect your feelings. Do this privately and be brutally honest with yourself. While shopping, use the list to spend extra money on the high-rated items and less money on low-rated items, opting for functional brands.

- Drill down. Break down the major categories of spending into subcategories to reveal more opportunities for savings. For example, a man might rate his work wardrobe as a three for psychological income. But more specifically, he evaluates his suit and ties as threes, his shirts as two and socks as one. The next time he goes shopping for work clothes he knows how to divvy up his money to get the greatest satisfaction from the purchases.

The simple exercise forces you to think critically about the types of purchases you care most about—those that give you something extra. If you don't get that additional boost, go for a cheaper brand and use the saved money elsewhere. Make PI a part of your everyday purchase-decision process.

Impulse Spending: Harness the Urge to Splurge

Americans today live a much more luxurious lifestyle than previous generations. But with new abundance comes a new set of problems grandma and grandpa didn't have. Among them is the overwhelming number of opportunities to spend impulsively.

In previous generations, consumers who saw an enticing advertisement at home often had to wait at least until the next day when they could withdraw money and get to the store. That provided a built-in cooling-off period that allowed the urge to pass. Or if they had no cash, they simply couldn't buy it.

That has all changed. Today, the availability of ATMs, easy credit, online shopping, and home-shopping TV networks provides the potential to be round-the-clock consumers who can satisfy buying urges immediately.

That lends itself to impulse spending that can derail the best of household financial plans.

Academic research suggests we only have a limited amount of willpower. This reservoir of self-control is regularly depleted and replenished. It's similar to exercising a muscle. When it's fatigued, it works less well until it recuperates.

So if we resist our impulses early in the day, for example, we are less likely to be able to resist something else later that day. Experiments show that people forced to exert self-control were later willing to spend more money for a product, buy more items, and spend more money than when their resistance was at full strength.

Because today's consumers are constantly bombarded with buying messages and offers of easy credit to buy things they can't afford, they need a deep supply of self-control. Otherwise, they succumb to impulse spending.

Here are ways to resist:

- Rest your "just say no" muscle. Don't expect that you can adhere to a strict food diet—a difficult self-control task—and avoid impulse purchases at the same time. If you're going shopping in the afternoon and will be tempted by impulse buys, spend the morning doing enjoyable activities that come easily to you. It's about choosing your battles and spacing them out.
- Avoid temptation. Different people require different amounts of self-control, depending on how intense the urge is. Someone

might require a lot of self-control to avoid impulse buys in an electronics store but may have little trouble rejecting the offer of an ice cream cone. Find your impulse-buying triggers and steer clear. That way, you don't need to tap your supply of self-control.

For example, if television advertising tempts you, consider recording your favorite TV shows and skipping commercials. If you Internet shop when you're bored, play a game on the computer instead.

Don't touch merchandise or try on clothes. Research shows physical contact with an item intensifies the temptation.

- Keep an eye on the prize. Setting detailed financial goals can help you avoid impulse spending. That way, you have specific reasons not to spend. It's easier to spend dollars not earmarked for anything in particular. During a supermarket shopping trip, for example, adhere to a shopping list, which represents your goals.

  An unrelated tip is to use the self-checkout. For some reason, retailers report much lower sales for impulse buys such as candy, batteries, and celebrity tabloid newspapers at self-checkout aisles, presumably because shoppers are busy scanning and bagging their groceries.

- Monitor your mood. Research shows that your mood can affect your ability to resist temptation. Oddly, both extremely good moods and bad moods can encourage impulse buying. More helpful is realizing times when you've had to bottle up your high or low emotions. That requires self-control, which depletes your reservoir and makes you vulnerable to your buying impulses.

- Use cooling-off tricks. Put some time and space between you and a would-be impulse buy. Place the item back on the shelf and wait 48 hours to determine whether you really want it, or at least put it back and take a trip around the store. For bigger-ticket items, avoid impulsively buying the item but promise yourself to go home, get on the Internet, and research the product's quality and compare prices. That could dampen the desire and can even lead to getting a lower price and avoiding troublesome products.

At the minimum, force your intellectual self to challenge the emotional self, with the questions, "Do I really need this?" and "Will I even want this item tomorrow?" Or try to substitute. Instead of buying a $300 handbag, treat yourself to an unplanned $4 fancy coffee to alleviate the urge to splurge.

- Get a do-over. If you succumb to an impulse purchase that you don't want, take advantage of the retailer's generosity—return the item ASAP.

No Excuses: The Lies We Tell Ourselves

A lousy attitude and self-deception are part of many poor spending decisions. Weak and whiny exclamations are nothing more than excuses for bad spending behavior.

An attitude adjustment can help. The following are quotations people use every day for doing dumb things with their money:

- "I could die tomorrow, so I'll live for today." This immature attitude justifies actions of the buy-it-now and pay-for-it-whenever class. It's the primary excuse for not saving money. The solution is to develop financial goals. That way you can see "tomorrow" in a more concrete way and have a reason not to go overboard on today's spending.

- "I work hard, I deserve it." This is akin to a four-year-old throwing a tantrum in the toy store crying, "Gimme, gimme." Many Americans are overworked, it's true. And, yes, you have to treat yourself occasionally. After all, enjoying money is one of the few things you can do with it.

   But *self-gifting*, as academics call it, is more prominent today, possibly because marketers are using it as a pitch to sell such products as day-spa services and right-hand diamond rings for women. Advertisers are quick to point out that you should buy their product "because you deserve it." Of course, you also deserve to live out a retirement that doesn't include regular helpings of Alpo.

- "I don't have a head for numbers." This is the excuse given for not paying attention to personal finances. But managing money doesn't require complicated mathematics. Besides the availability of cheap handheld calculators, consumers have a plethora of online tools to help with all sorts of financial planning. Go to www.dinkytown.com, for example, to see how easy they are to use. The biggest help to finances will be calculating exactly how much money is coming in, how much is going out, and where it's going. That involves grade-school addition and subtraction.

  You don't need to be expert in complicated financial concepts. In fact, many of the complications in personal finance—think whole life insurance, annuities, sector mutual funds—aren't good ideas for average consumers anyway. Accept the concept of "good enough." Be happy to do smart things with your money, even if they aren't the absolute best you can do. Often, the absolute best involves more risk than you should be taking.

- "I'm too busy to compare prices or manage money." This might be true for a small fraction of people, but mostly it's a lie. With easy-to-use personal finance software, the Internet to compare prices, and automatic savings and bill paying, it takes less time than ever to manage money. Shutting off the TV one night a week will provide most people plenty of time to manage their finances. For those truly time-strapped, consider hiring a good financial adviser. It's more expensive than managing finances yourself, but better than doing nothing.

- "It's an investment." Most consumer purchases are not investments. Investments are supposed to have a chance at being worth more in the future than they are today. Almost all consumer purchases plummet in value the moment you leave the store, a guaranteed loser of an "investment." So you don't "invest" in a car, a plasma TV, or a new pair of shoes unless somehow they'll make you money. They are expenses. Pacifying your spending guilt by calling them an investment is self-delusion.

- "I don't earn enough to save money." Saving is not about what you earn, it's about what you keep. The common advice to "pay yourself first" can help. It refers to setting aside a little money, preferably with an automatic paycheck or bank account withdrawal, before you start paying your bills. Paying yourself first might seem impossible until you try it. One way to save for retirement, for example, is to use a 401(k) plan at work and contribute the maximum to get the company match, often 6 percent of pay. If your paycheck truly only covers the cost of bare necessities, you have an income problem. It's time to work more hours or earn more with the hours you work. Do not use "pay yourself first" to save money at a low interest rate, when you have high-interest debt. In that case, paying yourself first would mean earmarking extra money for debt reduction.

- "People who think about money are greedy." You had better be thinking about money—a lot. No recent generation has had more responsibility for their own money management than today's Americans. Your parents or grandparents might have had defined pensions, which guaranteed them a retirement income. But somebody else managed that money. Today, we manage our own, in 401(k)s, IRAs, and other financial vehicles. Stock options and grants used to be for the highest-level executives. Today, hourly employees might receive them. With children living at home longer and elderly parents moving in, the "sandwich generation" has to provide for more people on the same income. Thinking about money isn't being greedy. It's about being a responsible adult.

Money Personalities: What Type Are You?

Researching big purchases, comparing prices, using coupons, and having a general knowledge about spending your money wisely matters little if you can't overcome emotional spending.

That concept might turn off some people, especially those who think personal finance is about numbers and math. But personal finance is often more personal than it is finance.

Marketers know it. With advertising, they can persuade consumers to buy things they don't need, or even want, by appealing to their emotions. Beer and soft drink marketers often show beautiful people having a great time, as if by consuming their product you too will be beautiful and have a great time.

Your feelings about money also play a role in your relationships with spouses and significant others. Money fights are often cited as a major factor in divorce in North America.

Often your bad money attitude can be traced to your parents, and unless the cycle is broken, will be handed down to your children. In that way, it's like an inherited money gene. It can affect your family tree for generations. Some people will mimic their parents' money habits. Others rebel.

In fact, recognizing your emotional triggers for earning, spending, and saving is a prerequisite for all other spending advice. To begin uncovering your emotional ties to spending money, ask yourself these questions:

- What personal experiences, good or bad, relating to money do you recall from childhood?
- Did you work for money as a teenager? Why or why not? What did you do with your money as a teen?
- How did your parents manage money? How did they handle a financial crisis? Did money cause tension in the family?
- What did your parents actively teach you about money? How much freedom did they give you to make money decisions?
- What role did money play in your career choice?
- What are your fears about money?
- Complete this sentence: "If I had a lot more money, I would…"

That simple quiz should shed some light on why you act the way you do with money. Further self-examination will also reveal you have a money type.

Much has been written on money personalities, and experts categorize them differently. Some describe six basic types, whereas others use nine or eight or four. The number of personalities doesn't matter as much as realizing you have one. And your money personality does-n't necessarily match your social personality. Your money personality is more likely to be influenced by your parents and upbringing. You either mimic your parents' money habits or rebel against them.

You should also know that money personalities take center stage in many marriages and other relationships. The consensus seems to be that opposite money personalities do, indeed, attract. Part of the challenge of marriage and other relationships is reconciling those clashing money types.

Below are descriptions of major money types. The goal is not to dramatically change your money type but to help you prosper with the one you have:

- The Joneses. In "keeping up with the Joneses," you are the Joneses but don't realize it. You're focused on achieving success and letting others know just how successful you are by buying lots of stuff. The Joneses equate money with success, or at least, it's the main way of keeping score. Ambition is the upside; overspending is the downside. The Joneses usually earn enough to have the nice playthings they want, but often think they can outearn their consuming stupidity. You should capital-ize on your money-making ability by keeping more of what you earn. Slow down and fit your "want" purchases into the rest of your financial priorities.

- Gamblers. You're the thrill-seeker and risk-taker with money. You often think you're smarter than the rest and are certain to make a big score. The upside is you're comfortable with risk, which can pay off handsomely with money. But untamed risk-taking is dangerous and can land you in financial ruin. Try to rein in your bet-the-farm instincts by, for example, investing in a stock mutual fund rather than individual stocks.

- Financial fugitives. You get a thrill from buying, which causes you to overspend and go in debt. Or you lost a source of income and use debt to pay for necessities. Either way, you quickly find yourself on the run from creditors. If there's an upside, it's that you know the pain of being in huge debt and may have developed the resolve to get out. Your weakness is you either overspend or underearn, and you turn to credit cards as the bailout. Cut up your cards, find a way to make more than the minimum payment and second-guess each purchasing decision. Others will need to reexamine their career path and earn more money.

- Cruisers. You may be coping or even thriving financially, but your money life is on cruise control. A lack of a money crisis has made you comfortable with the status quo. The upside is you're organized and responsible. But complacency means you're missing out on opportunities and greater prosperity. Shake things up and review your finances comprehensively. For example, set a goal for a cushier retirement and determine whether you're saving aggressively enough to reach it.

- Ostriches. You bury your financial head in the sand because you're uncomfortable with money, even confused, intimidated, or embarrassed by it. The upside is you're not consumed by the idea of accumulating and spending money, which allows you to focus on more important things in life. But you'll end up regretting total avoidance of your money problems and not setting financial goals. Use set-it-and-forget-it money strategies such as automatic bill-paying and automatic investment plans.

- Misers. You hoard money and miss out on the fun and good you can do with it. You're intensely afraid of losing money and exert a great deal of effort to spend less. You might live too far below your means, perhaps in a joyless existence. The upside is you're an excellent saver but at the expense of what else money is good for—spending, giving, and allowing money to make its own money. Dip your toe in higher-risk investments by moving some money out of ultraconservative places, such as bank certificates of deposit, into a mutual fund that tracks the Standard and Poor's 500 stock indexes. And plan a nice vacation. You've earned it.

Shopping Addiction: "Shop Till You Drop" Ain't Funny

The bumper stickers can be amusing: "Born to shop," "Shop till you drop," "I am a mall-aholic," and "I came, I saw, I did a little shopping."

But for some, the lighthearted catchphrases point to a serious problem of out-of-control spending. It can destroy relationships and plunge consumers and their families into overwhelming debt, even bankruptcy.

Some 24 million people suffer from compulsive shopping disorder, according to a Stanford University study. And about one-quarter of Americans have a compelling need to purchase that hasn't become destructive, according to other estimates. It can affect the rich and poor, women and men.

Compulsive spending results in buying things not for a need or even a want. It stems more from a desire to feel better, whether to feel more self-confident or to experience a temporary adrenaline rush, similar to a drug addict scoring a fix. The high is from the act of purchasing, rather than owning the purchased item.

Many Americans have spending addictions to varying degrees, with most being manageable. But it can be a serious problem if you recognize yourself or someone you know in the following questions, developed with help from Olivia Mellan, a former spend-aholic turned author, money coach, and psychotherapist.

- Do you spend money when you go shopping, regardless of whether you need anything?
- Do you buy things or take financial risks even when you can't afford to?
- When life gets stressful, do you seek consolation by spending money?

- Do you spend money to cheer yourself up when feeling anxious, depressed, or bored?
- Do you celebrate by rewarding yourself with a spending or gambling spree?

If you think you might have a serious spending problem, consider seeking psychological counseling to uncover the root of the problem or joining Debtors Anonymous at www.debtorsanonymous.org/ or call 781-453-2743.

If the problem has yet to become overly destructive, first admit there's a problem and track how you feel when you spend. That will help identify triggers for overspending. Then set a goal for where saved money would go, from a child's college tuition to buying a sailboat. That will give you a reason to resist your buy-it-now urges.

If you have a shopping compulsion, try these tips:

- Pay for purchases with cash, check, or debit card.
- Make a shopping list and buy only what is on the list.
- Avoid temptation. Stay away from garage sales, discount warehouses, and the mall. Allocate a specific amount to spend when you do visit a retail store. Avoid catalogs, and don't watch TV shopping channels.
- Window shop only after stores have closed. If you window shop during the day, leave your wallet at home.
- Take a walk or exercise when the urge to shop comes on.
- Get help. If you can't manage your shopping addiction yourself, don't hesitate to get professional help from a mental health professional. And consider a financial adviser, who can provide perspective on your finances and give you a reason to stop shopping.

3

What a Waste!:
Pet Peeves and Hot Buttons

One of the cardinal rules of spending smart is to stop wasting money. Although that can be achieved in hundreds of ways, some topics are more controversial than others.

This chapter is likely to contain at least one section that makes you mad. And that's okay. You can disagree and ignore the advice. But you should at least read the section and have good reasons to spend your hard-earned money on such follies as timeshare vacations, cigarette smoking, and bottled water.

Other areas of spending aren't necessarily controversial, but they annoy us all. They include buying ink-jet cartridge refills at prices that soon surpass the price of the printer, those wildly expensive college textbooks, and greeting cards that cost $5 a pop.

It's not that these specific topics are the only areas of wasteful and frustrating spending. But reading this chapter will give you general concepts about how to spend your money smarter. It will help you challenge the notion that you're just stuck paying ridiculous prices, no matter what the purchase.

So, this chapter addresses specific topics on both big one-time expenses and small expenses that can add up.

Either way, they are prime spending areas to examine and cut waste. And yes, they are a few of my own personal pet peeves.

Bottled Water: Tap into Savings

Money doesn't grow on trees but water does fall from the sky—for free. Yet, Americans likely spent in the neighborhood of $16 billion on bottled water in 2006.[1] Maybe it's no accident that naive spelled backward is Evian. Bottled water can easily cost $10 per gallon, many times the cost of gasoline. Meanwhile, plain tap water, which for generations has been a perfectly fine source of drinking water, costs about half a cent per gallon. For an interesting comparison, see Table 3.1.

TABLE 3.1 Bottled Versus Tap Water: Cost in Perspective

$2 bottled water (16 oz.)	$16/gallon
Tap water at home	0.5 cents/gallon
Gallons of tap water you can buy for $16	3,200
Bathtubs you can fill with 3,200 gallons	89

Note: Based on bathtub using 36 gallons to fill.

So, if bottled water costs thousands of times more, it must be special, right? It must really come from mountain springs or glaciers or the fountain of youth. Unlikely. The origin for a lot of bottled water, including such big names as Dasani and Aquafina, can be traced to municipal tap water. That's right. Big companies like Coca-Cola and Pepsi Co. run tap water through a filter, bottle it, and sell it to you at ridiculous prices.

Okay, then, bottled water must be safer than tap water, right? There's no evidence of that, either. In fact, federal regulations for the testing of tap water are stricter than testing requirements for bottled water. Tap water must be tested for safety several times a day. Bottled water must be tested once a month. Think about which is probably safer.

Fine. But bottled water tastes better, right? People claim that's true. But in a slew of blind taste tests, consumers typically can't tell the difference between bottled and tap.

Other arguments against bottled water:

- No fluoride. Bottled water doesn't have fluoride. Some people like the idea of eliminating it, but fluoride does prevent tooth decay.
- The environment. Mother Earth isn't thanking you for drinking bottled water, considering how much energy and crude oil it takes to manufacture plastic bottles, let alone the fuel consumed to transport bottled water by truck. By contrast, delivery of tap water comes by pipes using environment-friendly gravity.

But if you're dissatisfied with tap water, here are common objections and some alternatives to bottled water:

- Taste. Do yourself the favor of conducting a simple blind taste test to determine whether, in fact, you can tell the difference between your tap water and bottled. If you can detect an objectionable chlorine aftertaste, fill a pitcher with water and store it uncovered in the refrigerator overnight. This will allow the chlorine to dissipate and eliminate the aftertaste. You could also use a simple carafe filter or more extravagant filters that go on your faucet or under the sink. And many refrigerators today have filtered-water dispensers. All those choices will be cheaper than bottled water. The only option that is more expensive is delivered water for water-cooler dispensers, according to *Consumer Reports* magazine.

- Safety. Tap water is by and large safe. If you're concerned about the safety of your tap water, contact your water company or authority. Federal law requires them to provide consumers with a water-quality report each year by July 1. Yours might be online at www.epa.gov/safewater, or call the EPA's Safe Drinking Water Hotline at 800-426-4791. And if you have a temporary concern with the safety of tap water, you could boil it to remove many potentially harmful components.

- Health. Water is a healthful substitute for such beverages as sugar-laden soft drinks, juices, and sport drinks. It has no caffeine or calories. But that's true of any water—bottled, filtered, or tap. So health is not a reason to choose plain bottled water over other water. However, in certain on-the-run scenarios, bottled water could make good health sense. For example, if you're thirsty in a convenience store and determined to buy a drink, bottled water could be a better choice than soda, for example. You'll be vastly overspending no matter what you buy in a single serving. At least, water won't damage your health.

- Convenience. Turning on your home's faucet is exponentially easier than driving to the store, standing in line to check out, and lugging home bottled water. Instead of buying bottled water for when you're on-the-go, you could buy the most expensive, feature-laden refillable water bottle you can find. Fill it with tap water or filtered water, and you'll quickly recoup the cost of the water bottle and continue to reap savings.

- Status. This may be the real reason some people buy bottled water. If you derive self-esteem from carrying name-brand water, then judge for yourself how much that's worth. An alternative is to buy a case of name-brand water on sale or at a warehouse club and refill bottles with tap water. The people you're trying to impress won't know the difference, and you'll save a bundle.

You won't save big bucks solely by skipping bottled water, but it illustrates a broader point about eliminating lame excuses for buying things you don't need.

Junky Insurance: Extended Warranties and Other Insurance You Don't Need

If there's one main way to save money on insurance, it is to avoid overinsuring. You can do that by understanding a single concept: *Insurance is supposed to protect you from financial ruin, not minor money annoyances.*

Yet consumers are offered insurance regularly and for routine purchases. Extended warranties are one of the most prevalent forms of insurance—though technically not categorized as insurance. Some retailers make far more money on the extended warranty they sell you than on the purchased item. That's because it's almost pure profit. You pay through the nose for the warranty, and they rarely have to pay for a defective item. Today, you can insure your cell phone, your eyeglasses, and almost any purchase at an electronics store.

You can also insure your life against specific causes of death, including cancer, heart disease, or even accidents while traveling. Here's an easy rule of thumb for those types of insurances: Just say no. It's all junk.

Extended Warranties

Extended warranties are the first of the insurances you probably do not need. At best, extended warranties are a type of insurance that usually turns out to be a waste of money. At worst, the add-on warranties are cold-hearted rip-offs that play on the fears of consumers during a vulnerable moment at checkout. In nearly every case, extended warranties are a great deal for the salesperson, who receives a fat commission. And they're a bad deal for you because you're unlikely to use the warranty, and you're vastly overpaying for protection. See Table 3.2 for how profitable warranties are for electronics retailer Best Buy. In fact, you might say Best Buy is more in the business of selling warranties than electronics.

TABLE 3.2 Extended Warranty Case Study: Best Buy Electronics

2007 total profits	$1.38 billion
2007 profits from extended warranties	$790 million
% of company profits from extended warranties	57%

Source: *Minneapolis Star Tribune*, July 21, 2007

The scene is played out over and over again, especially at electronics stores. I witnessed one myself during the Christmas shopping season as a man of maybe 40 years old bought a computer. While processing the checkout, the youthful salesman asked the man if he wanted an extended warranty. Blindsided by the question, the man stammered a few seconds trying to process the question and decide. But before the customer could utter another, "Well,....uhhh," the salesman chimed in with an authoritative and well-rehearsed argument for buying the warranty. I was out of earshot, but the man's body language said it all. His shoulders and head drooped slightly. His head nodded. He had succumbed to one of the biggest rip-offs in retail today.

You might pay $300 for a digital camera and $60 for an extended warranty. That's 20 percent of the camera's cost, or like paying $5,000 for a warranty on a $25,000 car—a terrible deal. Besides, if it's defective you'll know right away. The store will take it back for free under its return policy. And the manufacturer warranty often covers the product for the first several months to a year. So, if you buy an extended warranty, you're betting that the item will break in a specific window of time—after the manufacturer warranty expires and before the extended warranty expires. You're also betting the repair will cost more than the price of the warranty. That's an improbable and pessimistic gamble, especially when so many products are reliable.

Other reasons not to buy extended warranties start with the cardinal rule of insurance—you don't insure against small financial problems, like a camera malfunctioning. Also, you might already get an extended warranty through your credit card, if you used the card to buy the item. And, you could self-insure by setting aside in a separate bank account all the money you would have spent on extended warranties. Tap that fund for repairs.

One further point is to never buy an extended warranty on a rapidly depreciating product. For example, a $200 warranty on a $1,000 computer becomes a lot less valuable in its third year when that computer might be worth just $200. In other words, at year number three you could simply buy the same computer new instead of getting it repaired. In this example, if you bought an extended warranty, you would have paid $200 to insure something worth $200.

Other insurances you probably do not need include

- Specific-death insurance. It doesn't matter whether you die from cancer, in a plane crash, or by alien abduction, you need life insurance to protect the people who rely on your income. And you'll need to cover all kinds of expenses, not just your mortgage and credit cards. So, skip cancer insurance, air travel insurance, credit card insurance, mortgage life insurance, and the rest of the specialty insurances. They only duplicate what should be covered by your term life policy.
- Child life insurance. If you think about it, this makes no sense. Virtually nobody depends on a child's income for financial security. So what's the point of getting an insurance payout in the unlikely event a child dies? If you would be financially devastated by funeral and burial costs, you could consider a small term life policy on a child.
- Rental-car insurance. First, your regular auto policy may cover rental cars; three-quarters of policies do. Second, if you pay by credit card, you may receive additional coverage as a standard benefit of the card. You need rental-car insurance; just don't pay for duplicate coverage.
- Credit card loss protection. Most credit cards don't hold you liable for any purchases a thief makes with a lost or stolen credit card. Others might charge you the federal limit of $50 if you don't report it right away—hardly insurance-worthy.

You do, however, need long-term disability insurance, which pays you if you're out of work for an extended time because of an illness or disability. It protects one of your most valuable assets—you're ability to earn an income. Getting group disability insurance through an employer will be far cheaper than getting an individual policy.

Timeshare Vacations: The Worst Real Estate Deal Ever

Going away on vacation is often among the highlights of any calendar year, but it can turn into a nightmare if you fall for high-pressure sales tactics and buy a vacation timeshare.

A *timeshare* is a right to use a vacation home, usually during the same earmarked week each year. The idea is that if you buy a time-share, you don't need to pay for a hotel or rental house when you go on vacation. And timeshares can be more luxurious than many rentals and hotels. They usually offer two bedrooms, a kitchen, and a clothes washer and dryer. Timeshares appeal to people who dream of owning a vacation home but can't afford one.

Consumers usually buy timeshares after lengthy, high-pressure pitches from timeshare salespeople. The pitches seem to be working. Timeshare sales in 2006 totaled $10 billion, up 81 percent over five years, according to the American Resort Development Association. All told that year, there were 4.4 million timeshare owners. The average price shelled out for these vacation weeks was $18,502. See Table 3.3 for how dramatically sales have increased.

TABLE 3.3   Timeshare Sales

Year	Sales (Billions)
2002	$5.5
2003	$6.5
2004	$7.9
2005	$8.6
2006	$10.0

Source: American Resort Development Association

Despite the popularity of timeshares, there are many good reasons not to buy them. Here are a few:

- It's a lousy investment. A timeshare will lose value from the moment you buy it. You would be fortunate to sell it for half price the day after you buy it.

- You usually can't unload it at all. Timeshares are notoriously difficult to sell, even if it's in a prime location and you're willing to take a loss. The Federal Trade Commission has warnings about timeshares, saying in part, "be aware that resales are difficult, if not impossible, because there's no secondary market."

- You keep on paying. Maintenance fees average $555 a year and rise annually. And you might have to pay separately for real estate taxes and special assessments for unexpected costs at the resort. You have to pay the fees every year, forever, regardless of whether you actually use the timeshare.

- It takes a while to break even. One of the attractions of a timeshare is you can lock in a price for your vacation lodging and don't have to deal with hotel rate inflation. But you will pay a lot of money upfront. It could literally take a decade or two before you even reach the break-even point and start to realize a financial benefit of a locked-in price. And that doesn't even include the opportunity cost—or what else you could have been doing with that money instead of making payments on a timeshare. Of course, all the annual fees you shelled out over the years erode your savings.

- You lose vacation flexibility. Timeshare resorts like to highlight how easy it is to trade your unit for timeshares elsewhere. But it's often a huge hassle and could require vacation planning a year in advance. Trading costs paid to a timeshare-swap company involve an annual fee of about $100 and a per-transaction fee of up to about $150. Also, if you have a slow-season timeshare in Pennsylvania's Poconos, for example, don't expect to trade for a prime week in Maui.

You don't have to believe me that timeshares are a terrible purchase. Believe these real timeshare owners who emailed me after I wrote about timeshares in my national column, "Spending Smart," published in Tribune Co. newspapers:

"Help! We have a timeshare and don't know how to get rid of it. We know that we will not get our money back, but we don't know where to turn."

"Do you have any suggestions after the damage has been done, as far as unloading this beast?"

"I simply want out of this timeshare, even if it means forfeiting my initial investment and assessments paid to date."

If you still think a timeshare is for you, at least buy one second-hand and let the initial owner get soaked on the depreciation. You can buy it for pennies on the dollar, and plenty are available, no matter where you want to vacation. If you're not paying cash for the time-share, it might be a good sign that you can't afford it.

If you already own a timeshare and are desperate to get out, don't pay an upfront listing fee to someone promising to sell your time-share. You're unlikely to get any results. Your best bets for dumping a timeshare are to sell it back to the resort—although, that seldom works—or advertise it online or in local newspapers or vacation mag-azines. You could also donate it to a charity and at least get a tax deduction and escape the obligation of annual fees.

More information on ridding yourself of a timeshare is available at various Web sites, including the Timeshare Trap, www.timesharetrap.com.

Smoking: Your Money, Up in Smoke

A decision about $3 million is a big deal, even to the richest among us. The decision to smoke cigarettes is even bigger.

Here's how: A pack-a-day smoker will spend about $2,000 a year on cigarettes, which is $5.50 a pack times 365 days in a year.

If that person smokes from age 18 through age 65 and the price of cigarettes never goes up, he will have spent $96,000 on cigarettes.

That sounds like a lot—that is, until you examine the opportunity cost, or what else he could have done with his cigarette money. If he instead put that $2,000 a year in a Roth Individual Retirement Account (IRA) that earned an 11 percent return, he would accumulate $3 million in tax-free cash at age 65. Three million dollars!

Hope he liked the smokes.

That shows how smoking is a lousy habit, even before considering the obvious health problems it causes for smokers and people around them.

Still, one in five adults—or some 45 million Americans—smokes cigarettes, according to the Centers for Disease Control. And smokers spent $82 billion on cigarettes in 2005. Unfortunately, statistics show those most likely to smoke are those who can least afford it. Thirty percent of people living below the poverty level are smokers. And smoking is highly correlated with education. For example, more than 43 percent of adults with a General Education Development (GED) diploma smoke, compared with just 7 percent for those with a graduate college degree.

Smokers certainly have the right to spend their money on cigarettes and enjoy their habit. But they should know that smoking can break you financially and cost your family long after you're prematurely dead. That $3 million decision by an 18-year-old to smoke is just the beginning of the financial hardship. Consider the following

- Collateral spending. The cost of cigarettes alone is not the only expense. Insurances are much costlier for smokers. Life, health, even homeowners insurance premiums will all be more expensive. Other costs are more difficult to measure, but you can imagine spending more than nonsmokers on teeth cleaning and whitening, dry cleaning, and replacing clothes and furniture marred by cigarette burns. Then there's the lower resale value of vehicles and homes because they smell of smoke, which may total literally thousands of dollars over a lifetime. Smokers also tend to be less productive at their jobs and spend more on health care. In 1999, the CDC estimated the cost to the average smoker in the hidden expenses of health care and lost productivity alone totaled $7.18 per pack.

- Your career. Employers in some states have actually fired employees who smoke, even if they smoke only during non-work hours. Other employers have vowed not to hire smokers in the first place. In 2005, the National Workrights Institute estimated that more than 6,000 companies refused to hire smokers. Employers cite higher health-care costs for smokers and lost productivity at work.

- Return on quitting. Business people always want to know the return on investment, or ROI, for money they spend. The ROI on investing in a smoking cessation program is a no-brainer, if it helps you quit. Over-the-counter nicotine replacement systems, whether gum, lozenges, or patches, cost $4 to $5 a day. Meanwhile, many smokers easily spend more than that daily for cigarettes. So, paying for treatment is actually cheaper than smoking. Then you reap the big savings after you've quit for good. Of course, quitting cold-turkey may be more difficult, but it's absolutely free. Then the ROI is a return on your investment of effort and self-discipline.

- Cost to your family. Besides the obvious harm to your family from secondhand smoke—which costs nonsmoking Americans nearly $6 billion a year, according to the American Academy of Actuaries—your family is paying for your habit in other ways. If you're a breadwinner in the family, your likelihood for premature death starts kicking in during your late 40s and early 50s, your prime income-earning years. That robs your survivors of whatever income and greater inheritance they might have had if you had quit sooner. And through the years, all those thousands of dollars spent on smoking could have instead been spent on family vacations. Or it could have led to lower financial stress and greater family harmony.

And if a child picks up the habit because mom or dad smoked, you've passed the financial curse to a new generation.

Ink-Jet Cartridges: Refill Rage

Gasoline is the liquid whose price seems to infuriate Americans most. But quickly gaining on consumers' rage scale is the price of ink-jet printer refills.

The cumulative cost of ink-jet refills can quickly surpass the cost of the printer itself. And that's the business model used by printer makers. It's like the razor-blade model, where they practically give you the razor and make big profits on the blade replacements.

But you're not stuck paying ridiculous prices for name-brand ink cartridges. You have alternatives, although there's a trade-off between price and quality. Studies show the printer's manufacturer makes the best-quality inks for any given printer. Nevertheless, you don't always need top quality.

If you're printing out an email, driving directions, or your child's grade-school project on regular copy paper, you probably don't need the absolute best quality. You might not even need top quality when printing digital photos. If the photo fades after time because of using a lesser-quality ink, you could always print it again.

One of the best alternatives for printing snapshots is to let someone else do it. Using a photo-finisher at various retailers, including Wal-Mart and many chain drugstores, provides excellent quality at a cheaper price than you can print them yourself. *Consumer Reports* found that photo finishers charge 15 cents to 25 cents for a 4-by-6-inch print, whereas printing at home costs 25 cents to 40 cents.

Another idea is to use two computer printers. For text, use a black-and-white laser printer, which will give you comparatively cheap printouts. For photos, use a color printer with high-quality ink or a small dedicated snapshot printer.

If you like the convenience of printing at home and regularly will be buying ink-jet refills, your options are presented in the following list in descending order of price and ink quality. This list was developed after an extensive interview with Charles Brewer, managing editor of *The Hard Copy Supplies Journal*, a publication by imaging industry market-research firm Lyra Research.

- **Brand names.** If you must have the absolute best quality, use ink and paper that match your printer, whether Hewlett-Packard, Canon, Lexmark, or others. You'll get the most accurate colors, and the print is less likely to fade. This is the most expensive option, so compare prices online and in stores. Compare the unit price of inks because some lower-priced cartridges might just contain less ink.

- **Store brands.** These cartridges are offered by such names as OfficeMax, Office Depot, and Rhinotek. The print quality will likely be good, but they are more susceptible to fading than brand-name inks.

- **Refill stores.** Such franchised retail shops as Cartridge World and Caboodle Cartridge allow you to bring in your old cartridge to be refilled or swapped with a different refilled cartridge.

- **Refill machines.** These are cartridge-refill machines in such stores as Walgreens and OfficeMax. The machines use a limited number of inks that may or may not match your printer well, so there may be some trial and error.

- **Refill kit.** Do-it-yourself refill kits can contain quality ink, but it's a messy chore to transfer ink to your cartridge. And a word about all refills, whether from a do-it-yourself kit, refill shop, or machine: An ink cartridge can only be refilled four to ten times with any of these refill methods. After that, the print head could burn out.

- **Online generics.** If a generic replacement for your $45 cartridge costs $7 online, there's a reason, Brewer said. You just can't count on the quality of the ink and the cartridge, which may leak. Batches of the same cartridges might differ in quality.

So, how do you choose? One idea is to start with store brands, and each time you need refills drop a level in quality to save money. Ask yourself whether you notice a difference. If the quality becomes so inferior, it's not worth the savings, go up a level in quality, and you've found your ink-jet comfort zone—your ideal trade-off between quality and price.

One additional warning: Wherever you buy cartridges, don't buy too many at a time. Cheap printers break easily. If you have to replace it, you might be stuck with a box full of cartridges that won't fit any current-model printer.

And a dirty little secret of the industry is this: Your printer lies. It will tell you it's running out of ink long before it really is. For example, a 2007 study commissioned by printer-maker Epson, revealed that multi-ink systems used less than 60 percent of the ink before the cartridge had to be replaced. And multi-ink printers aren't alone. You can remove, shake, and replace all ink-jet and laser-jet cartridges and potentially get hundreds more pages out of them.

Lottery: Winning the Jackpot Isn't a Financial Plan

Playing the lottery can be fun. It can provide the fantasy of hitting a jackpot and all the house-on-the-beach and red-sport-car images you can conjure.

But it's a bad use of your spending money. Even more so if you're an avid ticket-buyer and you secretly count on winning the lottery to finance your retirement or compensate for your financial despair. A survey cosponsored by the Consumer Federation of America showed many Americans with low and moderate incomes believed they had a better chance of building a $500,000 nest egg for retirement by playing the lottery than by saving and investing.

Lotteries are known, ungraciously, as a tax on the stupid. That's a little harsh. More accurately, lotteries are a tax on the hopeless. Only someone with no prospects would resort to such lousy odds for anything more than fun and whimsy.

There really aren't any tips for not playing the lottery. Just don't. But here are some interesting facts about the probability of winning one of those big lottery jackpots. They might persuade you to spend your money elsewhere.

- You're five times more likely to die in an automobile crash driving to the store to buy a lottery ticket than to win the jackpot.
- The probability of winning a major jackpot is about 1 in 150 million to 1 in 175 million. The chance of dying by snake bite this year is significantly better, 1 in 96 million, according to the U.S. National Safety Council.
- You're more likely to become president of the United States or a Catholic saint, at least according to the odds.
- Take an example of a relatively small lottery, where you have a 1 in 14 million chance of winning. The odds of winning the small lottery are the same as plunking down a dollar and betting you can repeatedly flip a coin and have it come up heads 24 times in a row, according to calculations by Fred Hoppe, professor of mathematics and statistics at McMaster University in Hamilton, Ontario. Take a coin out of your pocket and start flipping to get a sense of how unlikely that is. Don't forget to plunk a dollar on the table each time.

If instead of playing the lottery every day, a person put $1 a day into a growth mutual fund earning 12 percent per year from birth to age 65, they would amass $5 million. Though not a huge lottery jackpot, it's a nice sum of money.

And it's far more likely than winning the lottery.

Textbooks: Get Schooled in the Alternatives

As if college tuition wasn't expensive enough, college textbook prices have soared. Some students are spending more than $1,000 per year. Many books cost more than $100 each.

Rising prices are even more irritating when textbook publishers frequently—and sometimes unnecessarily—revise editions, making older ones obsolete. Adding CD-ROMs and study materials the professor doesn't require—and won't use—boosts textbook prices.

But you're not necessarily stuck paying outrageous prices at the campus bookstore. You can spend less—maybe even hundreds of dollars less—with a little planning and effort. To cut spending on textbooks, here are some ideas aside from the obvious tip to buy used books from the campus bookstore, which may be in short supply:

- Plan ahead. Find out what books you really need, even by contacting the professor if you can't find out online or through the bookstore. Don't get the optional books until you know you'll read them. Get the 10-digit ISBN code. It's easier to shop for books by number than title. You could also buy previous editions of the book if the professor approves.

- Get the book free. Sometimes students can study from textbooks on reserve at the campus library, although students won't have the convenience of using the books anytime they want, and they can't mark in the books. English majors especially can benefit from downloading free classic novels that are out of copyright protection. For example, you can download *Pride and Prejudice* by Jane Austen or *Moby Dick* by Herman Melville via such Web sites as Project Gutenberg, www.gutenberg.org. Free study guides are available at SparkNotes, www.sparknotes.com. Another free way to get books is to swap them with other students on campus or at www.campusbookswap.com.

- Shop online. Buying books online gives you a wider selection of used books and better prices on new ones. If you order from an out-of-state vendor, you might also avoid state sales tax. Check such Web sites as Amazon.com, eBay.com, Abebooks.com, and BestBookBuys.com. Order early enough to leave time for processing and shipping, and read the return policy.

- Shop early. You'll get the best deals because you'll have time to research the best prices and choose from the largest quantity of used books. And when shopping online, a retailer is less likely to bungle your purchase during a slow period, as opposed to when it is swamped with orders near the start of school. Also, you will have time to choose the cheapest shipping option, which sometimes is free if you're willing to wait a couple weeks.

- Strip down the book. If you have a choice, skip the bundled study materials, such as CD-ROMs and study guides, unless you know your professors will use them or highly recommend them. Often they won't. Look for textbooks that are available in softcover and black-and-white versions, which are less expensive.

- Buy overseas. International editions are often the same books but cheaper—and wildly cheaper if used. Check return policies, if you think you might need to return the book.

- Save receipts. If it turns out your instructor doesn't really use the text or you end up quickly dropping the class, return the book for a refund. Of course, that assumes you didn't write in the book or highlight it.

- Sell early. If you can finish studying for finals before everyone else, you'll have a better chance of selling back the book if the bookstore is accepting a limited number of book buybacks. But you may receive more money by selling it yourself in person or online.

Hybrid Vehicles: Have a Nonfinancial Reason for Buying One

Driving a hybrid car or truck makes sense for several reasons. Typical reasons are helping the environment, helping the United States break its dependence on foreign oil, and helping yourself save money on gasoline.

But the last one, saving money, is a bit of a fallacy. Yes, you save money on gasoline. But you have to pay such a premium to buy a hybrid car that you're unlikely to recoup that extra money in gas savings—at least during the first five years of ownership.

That was the conclusion of *Consumer Reports* in 2006, when it did the math on several hybrid vehicles. In that study, just two small hybrids, the Toyota Prius and Honda Civic Hybrid actually saved enough money in gasoline over five years to warrant the added expense—and those models barely made it worthwhile.

Since that report, the hybrid market has continued to evolve. But even if the price premium declines for buying hybrids over gasoline-only models in the coming years, you'll have many considerations if cost savings is your primary goal. They include

- Higher cost. Hybrids can cost thousands of dollars more than their gas-only counterparts, which means paying more sales tax and more interest if you're financing the vehicle. And as of this writing, hybrids were in high demand relative to production, which means dealers are less likely to give big discounts off sticker price.

- Your mileage may vary. For years, the window-sticker mileage estimates, sanctioned by the Environmental Protection Agency, have been inflated, with few consumers able to achieve the listed miles per gallon. Those numbers will change in 2008 to better reflect real-world driving conditions. But it doesn't matter what that number says; what matters is the mileage you achieve. So, if you do a lot of highway driving, where hybrids are less helpful on mileage, your breakeven point for recouping the hybrid price premium extends further into the future.

- Tax credits. You might have heard about lucrative tax credits you can get for buying a hybrid vehicle. Unfortunately, those credits expired, and hybrid buyers in 2008 aren't likely to get a similar break unless Congress acts. Those credits were included in the *Consumer Reports* study. Without tax credits, hybrids are even less likely to make good financial sense.

- Depreciation. All vehicles depreciate from the moment you buy them. And hybrids depreciate in value faster than gas-only models.

- Ongoing costs. Hybrids cost slightly more to insure and maintain. These aren't primary considerations, but it adds to the burden a hybrid has to overcome before being a financially prudent buy.

If you're buying a hybrid vehicle on principle, that's fine. Just know what it's really costing you. And a plus for hybrids is they tend to be very reliable, which is worth something in dollars, and hybrid owners tend to be very satisfied with their purchases. But don't buy a hybrid strictly for what it can save your pocketbook. You and your pocketbook are likely to be disappointed.

Greeting Cards Discarded: Special-Occasion Cardboard Rethought

Sending a greeting card on holidays, birthdays, anniversaries, and other occasions has long been a nice tradition. The cardboard greetings can say such momentous things as, "I'm thinking about you," "I'm proud of you," or "I love you."

But the cards are not cheap, often pushing past $4 each, if purchased individually. And after you plunk down the money and take the time to add postage to mail the card, you wonder whether all that effort and expense was even appreciated.

Americans spend nearly $7.5 billion on greeting cards each year, according to the Greeting Card Association. The 90 percent of households that send cards buy an average of 30 individual cards a year. Add sales tax, postage, and boxed cards, and total household spending on greeting cards could easily near $150.

That's not a make-or-break total for most families' finances, but it's enough to question whether buying greeting cards is worth it, or to at least examine less-expensive alternatives.

The rub is to reduce greeting-card spending without appearing cheap or disrespectful to family and friends accustomed to receiving cards from you. The key is judging your audience. Cards accompanying a gift to an elementary-school child will be quickly discarded. Yet, a mother might treasure a greeting card as a gift. Your brother might give the card a quick read and immediately trash it. An etiquette-conscious grandmother might be hurt if a birthday card never arrives.

So, you have to judge the value a recipient places on receiving a traditional greeting card. Here are ways to cut the cost of greeting cards without looking too cheap:

- Plan ahead. The most expensive way to send greetings is to leave card shopping to the last minute and dash into a Hallmark store for a last-minute fix. Most of the time, there's no excuse. Your brother's birthday and your wedding anniversary are not unexpected events. Mark your calendar with important birthdays and holidays, and then back up a week and add a reminder to buy a greeting card. Then you have the time to shop for an inexpensive card or seek alternative greetings.

- Personalize. Mailing a store-bought card that you simply sign is impersonal, regardless of how much you spent on it. The recipient might appreciate it more if it contains a handwritten note, even if it's a cheaper card. That only costs a few minutes of your time.

- Don't pay full price. Check out discount stores, dollar stores, and wholesale clubs that may sell last year's cards. Birthday and holiday wishes don't change much in a year. Look for deals on seasonal cards on sale after the holiday.

- Buy in bulk. Buying boxes of cards can dramatically cut the cost-per-card. Buy cards with universal designs and greetings, and then personalize them with a handwritten note.

- Send e-cards. Electronic cards are sent by email—or more often, an Internet web link to the card is sent to the recipient by email. A variety of online vendors offer such cards and let you customize a message. Many e-cards contain sound and animation. Although some e-cards are free, you have to pay for others, sometimes through a subscription of, say, $14 a year for an unlimited number of cards. But if you can send most of your cards electronically, that would be cheaper than buying paper cards. A side benefit offered by many e-card sites is a reminder service that alerts you to send an e-card when an event nears. And they offer delayed delivery of cards, so you can choose the card and schedule it to be automatically emailed later.

Try such Web sites as Americangreetings.com, Hallmark.com, 123greetings.com, Regards.com, and Greeting-cards.com.

- Make it yourself. Do-it-yourself cards don't need to be time-consuming. Creative and artistic people won't have a problem assembling a homemade card from craft materials available around the house. For others, relatively inexpensive computer software packages for $15 to $50 help create professional-looking paper cards. The software is generally easy to use and comes with hundreds of template cards you can customize. The cards come out looking nice—although not glossy—on a regular color ink-jet printer. You just need to buy card stock and envelopes. The cost per card is lower than most store-bought cards. And several Web sites, including American-Greetings.com, allow you to design and customize cards online and print them. Digital photography buffs can use the computer to create a photo card with an overlaid text message, which makes a nice greeting.

- Pick up the phone. With low long-distance phone rates, calling someone on a special occasion may not only be cheaper than a card but more appreciated. Five dollars could buy a nice greeting card and postage stamp. Or $1 buys a 20-minute long-distance phone conversation at 5 cents a minute. Of course, many cell phone plans include free long-distance calls.

1. $16 billion is an approximation derived from $10.9 billion in wholesale sales as reported by the Beverage Marketing Corp. plus a 50 percent markup at retail.

4

The Big Picture:
Strategies for Spending Smart

Spending can be like the game of chess. Most every chess game is different. But proficient players have learned both specific tactics and overall strategies for gaining advantage. Even if they have never seen an exact position before, they recognize familiar patterns in different sections of the board.

So it is with spending. Universal guidelines can govern how we spend our money, even if the details are different. Tactics to win retail skirmishes and overall strategies to win with money can be learned.

Some strategies in this chapter will be immediately recognizable, such as comparison shopping, tracking your spending, and buying items secondhand. Though some topics are familiar, they are powerful. Other topics will surely contain advice you haven't heard before.

So read on to develop strategies to force a checkmate in your battle to spend smarter.

Comparison Shopping: What's a Good Price?

Comparison shopping is fundamental to spending money smarter. Paying more than you have to just isn't logical, especially in a time when comparing prices is so easy and fast.

Accepting the first price you see is making a decision to be powerless. You're deciding to buy something based on nothing more than a trust that the seller is offering a fair price. You often have no reference point for whether the offered price is good or bad.

The fundamental point is this: Prices vary, sometimes significantly, on the exact same items. Here are tips on comparison shopping:

- Don't overvalue your time. People like to compare time spent saving money to their working-hour rate of pay. For example, someone who earns $20 an hour likes to say an hour-long task to save $15 isn't worth his time. But that's only true if during that hour the person could have—and would have—worked to get the $20. Otherwise, the comparison should properly be a $15 savings versus zero dollars in earnings. Additionally, even if you would have worked that hour, the fact that your $20 in earnings is subject to income taxes further deflates the argument.

  A 2002 study at Virginia Tech University used students to comparison shop for various purchases. In one case, 16 minutes of comparing prices on the same model of color television saved $100. That works out to $375 an hour.

  In a 2003 study, researchers were shocked to learn that *cherry pickers*—consumers who shopped multiple supermarkets to get good grocery deals—were not ridiculous cheapskates. Their savings more than made up for their investment of time, according to the study's authors, Stephen Hoch, a marketing professor at the Wharton School of the University of Pennsylvania, and Edward Fox, a marketing professor at Cox School of Business at Southern Methodist University.

I felt like I got a good deal on a new laser printer for my home office. The $129 price of the printer was pretty good, but then I needed a cord to hook it to my computer. That alone cost $35 at my local big-box electronics store. Then I remembered a local dollar store carried a variety of computer cords. Sure enough, I got a printer cord for $1 and returned the $35 cord. The cheaper cord worked great. Stopping by the dollar store was certainly worth my time.

Of course, paying for the convenience of not comparison shopping is a personal choice, and it's true that your free time is worth something in dollars. But ask yourself how much you're willing to pay for that convenience. What else could you have purchased with all the money you could have accumulated if you weren't constantly being overcharged?

• Go online. By using the Internet, you can regularly find better value and reduce the investment of time spent comparison shopping. Consumers can quickly research the type of product they should buy. Consumer Reports online, www.consumer-reports.org, and a host of other Web sites offer reviews of products and services. To get a better price, use shopping-comparison sites, called *shop-bots*. Plug in specific model numbers of products at such Web sites as Froogle.com, MySimon.com, Shopzilla.com, DealTime.com, and Shopping.com.

Even if you don't want to make a purchase online, you'll see a variety of prices and be able to recognize a competitive price. You could even use that knowledge as leverage to haggle for a better price from a bricks-and-mortar merchant.

• Realize small savings add up. It's true that a one-time savings of a few cents or even a few dollars might not be worth your time spent comparison shopping. But repeat purchases in large quantities add up in a hurry. Grocery shopping is a good example. Consumers often disregard prices on grocery items that cost just a few dollars because the nickel-and-dime savings seems small. But when those small savings are applied over and over again to dozens of items in your grocery cart, you're soon talking about real money. Saving 30 cents on an item bought each week becomes annual savings of nearly $16. Multiplied by 50 items, you're talking about $800 a year savings.

- Beware of retail gimmicks. Retailers can make it more difficult to comparison shop or try to reduce the incentive to compare prices. For example, many retailers offer a price-matching guarantee, where they will refund 110 percent of the price if you find the item cheaper elsewhere. Research shows such a guarantee might be a sign the retailer actually has higher-than-average prices. Many people will feel reassured by the guarantee and simply assume they are getting the lowest price. They never bother to compare prices after their purchase, and therefore don't cash in on the guarantee.

  Other tricks include end-of-aisle display items that aren't really on sale and reference pricing, where a sign might say an item usually costs $99.99 and is now $59.99—whether it's true or not. Mail-in rebates seem to lower the price but often don't. That's because consumers never bother to wade through the confusing instructions to submit rebate paperwork. And some retailers change model numbers on products, making it more difficult to comparison shop, even though their product is widely available.

- Test yourself. If you're unconvinced that comparison shopping is worth your time, conduct an experiment. Recall prices on several of your most recent expensive purchases. Then go online to a shop-bot, a site that combs the Internet providing users with product prices, and plug in the model numbers. Note the wide range of prices. How does the price you paid rank? By how much did you overpay? How long did it take you to find a significantly lower price? Now ask, "Would comparison shopping have been worthwhile?" The most likely answer is a definite yes.

Tracking Spending: Forensics on Your Finances

Before you can cut wasteful spending, you have to know where the money is going. So tracking your spending is a first step toward getting a handle on your personal finances.

The process is a bit like the popular *CSI* television programs, where crime-scene investigators look for clues that lead to the capture of the killer. With spending tracking, you collect clues about where your money is going to find out what's killing your finances.

This is not about the dreaded "B" word—*budget*. Creating a budget and sticking to it can be an immediate turnoff, and for good reason. It requires a level of diligence many people aren't willing to exert, especially if they're just starting to pay attention to their money.

The point is to know where your money is going, so you can redirect spending to fit your priorities. For example, buying a $3 latte every weekday morning and a $7 lunch at work seems harmless, until you scrutinize and total that spending. That's when you realize it amounts to roughly $2,500 a year. If you made coffee at home and brown-bagged it, you might be spending closer to $500 a year. That $2,000 difference could be spent on something you care more about, even if it's a vacation in the Caribbean.

So tracking spending isn't some exercise in overly conscientious personal finance. It allows you to plug the leaks of wasteful spending and redirect money to your true priorities. And it will prove how little expenses add up.

The good news is you don't have to do this tracking forever, although that would be ideal. Track daily spending for two months, realizing that you'll miss out on some seasonal expenses, such as air conditioning or summer vacation.

Persuade all the spenders in the family to participate, including spouses and children. It's a worthwhile exercise, and most people will discover several areas of wasteful spending that shock them.

And know this: Your day-to-day spending decisions will impact your finances more than any investment decision you will ever make.

Here are ideas for tracking spending:

- Keep receipts. This might be the simplest and best tactic. Ask for and keep receipts for all purchases. Designate a spot for all the little slips of paper. In just a few weeks, some disturbing spending patterns are likely to become obvious, without even totaling the receipts. Also keep all the billing statements that come in the mail, such as the electric bill, phone bill, and credit card statements.

  The receipt method might be best if you have a reluctant spouse who's wary about the exercise of expense tracking. At the least, he or she would probably be willing to dump daily receipts into a kitchen drawer.

- Track on paper. If you can carry a small notebook, jot down all purchases. Or keep a piece of paper clipped to your charge cards to log transactions.

- Write checks. A checkbook comes with a register to record purchases. But you'll have to combine this method with another, because personal checks are not universally accepted. If you're bad about recording checks, get the kind of checkbook that has duplicate pages.

- Use software. Quicken, Microsoft Money, a spreadsheet, or personal digital assistant (PDA) software all allow you to record spending and do some analysis that might be quicker than with pencil and paper. Be sure to avoid GIGO, or Garbage In, Garbage Out. It's a computer term that refers to bad data going into an analysis, which messes up the conclusions. The same is true of expense tracking. The most obvious area is cash spending. It doesn't help much to have a huge category of spending called "cash." You should break this down into what the cash is spent on for a truer picture of spending. Save ATM receipts and with a pen, make notes about cash spending on the back of the receipt.

- Use cards only. Using a debit or credit card for purchases is helpful because all your transactions are available in a single place—your bank statement or credit card bill. However, the credit card idea is a bad one for people who carry a revolving balance. Those people would be better off spending cash and tracking it.

After recording spending for a month, compile the expenses into categories and total them. This is a crucial step. Repeat after the second month.

When the surprise wears off that you're spending $80 a month on convenience-store soft drinks, $200 a month on eating out, and $300 a month on smoking cigarettes—or whatever expenses pertain to your life—resolve to funnel your money to things you really care about.

If the money-tracking exercise goes well, you might be a candidate to create a full-fledged budget. That means graduating from discovering where your money went in the past to telling your money where to go in the future.

A budget is not a restriction. In fact, a budget is about having more—more of the things that are important to you and more control. If you find your budget isn't reflecting your real spending or your real priorities, you can change it.

You might even find money for something you love that you didn't think you could afford, which really casts budgeting in a positive light. Maybe it's quitting a job and staying home with the kids, buying a home, completing a house improvement, buying a big-screen TV, or vacationing in Europe.

Budgets aren't complicated. You allocate money to different categories of expenses and then agree not to exceed those specified amounts. After tracking spending for a couple months, you should have an idea of how much to allocate to each category. And, of course, you'll have to keep tracking to know whether you're spending more or less than your budget allows.

A few examples of budget forms available online include www.consumercredit.com/budget-sheet.htm; the Microsoft Excel Web site, www.office.microsoft.com (click the Templates tab); and www.moneypurposejoy.com.

Rules of Thumb: Benchmarks for Spending Smart

Know-it-all experts in the financial world pooh-pooh rules of thumb, contending that everybody's money situation is unique. That's true to an extent, but good rules of thumb can be powerful.

First, rules of thumb are so easy that people uncomfortable with money topics might be encouraged to examine their spending. Second, the rules can provide perspective about your money and give you ideas to restructure your spending and saving habits.

Some savings rules of thumb are fairly well known, such as having an emergency fund of three to six months of expenses and contributing 10% to 15% of pay to retirement savings. The following are a few spending rules of thumb to consider. Take them with a grain of salt, especially if your situation is different from the typical American's. But they are quick benchmarks against which you can measure your own spending:

- Overall spending. One rule of thumb is the basis of *All Your Worth: The Ultimate Lifetime Money Plan*, a 2005 book by Harvard University professor Elizabeth Warren and her daughter, Amelia Warren Tyagi. In it, the authors suggest you should spend half your after-tax income on "must-haves," 30 percent on "wants," and 20 percent on savings. To calculate your after-tax income, add to your regular take-home pay employee and employer contributions to your 401(k), which is allocated to savings, and your portion of health insurance costs, which is allocated to must-haves.

What goes in each category might not be obvious. For example, the "must-haves" is a desperation-type budget, like you might live on after you've lost a job and were circling the financial wagons. Clothes, cable TV, and cell phone service fall into the wants category. Paying off debt counts as savings.

It's a useful exercise to tally your own spending to see how it breaks down, compared with the 50/30/20 formula. Many people will find their must-have commitments much higher than 50 percent.

- House. Your mortgage payment and associated costs should not exceed 29 percent of your gross monthly income. This includes mortgage principal and interest, real estate taxes, and homeowner's insurance, the usual items included in a monthly mortgage payment. An even simpler rule is the total mortgage should not be more than 2.5 times your gross income.

- Debt. Total debt payments should not exceed 36 percent of gross income. This includes the monthly payments for such items as mortgage, automobile loan, credit cards, student loans, and alimony. Keep in mind that the debt rules of thumb are ceilings. A healthier household budget would spend far less on debt. The Federal Housing Administration, the government agency that helps people buy homes by guaranteeing loans, allows up to a 41 percent total debt load, but that's quite hefty—and risky.

- Car. This may be the most shocking calculation for most people. Your car or truck payment shouldn't exceed 7 percent of your gross income—less if you have other debt. This derives from the previous two numbers: 36 percent total debt, minus 29 percent mortgage debt, leaves you 7 percent maximum for auto loans. And that assumes no credit card debt, student loan debt, or other obligations. So, a household with $80,000 in income and 29 percent mortgage debt can, at most, afford auto loans totaling $467 per month. That gets you a $19,500 car, assuming a 7 percent loan over four years. To recap, a household making a healthy income of $80,000 and being debt-free except for the mortgage can afford payments on one car costing less than $20,000, which means that household can't come close to buying most new cars.

- Car repairs. If the repair costs less than half of the trade-in value of the vehicle, repair it. Otherwise, sell it and buy another car. So, if a car's trade-in value is $3,000 and the repair costs less than $1,500, it's worthwhile—or at least worthy of serious consideration. You can find trade-in values online at kbb.com, edmunds.com, and nada.com.

- Holiday gifts. Spend no more than 1.5 percent of your gross income on the holidays, including gifts, decorations, travel, wrapping paper—everything. That means a household with $40,000 in income would spend $600, while a $100,000 household would spend $1,500. If you have a lot of consumer debt, you should consider spending less than 1 percent.

- Life insurance. A breadwinner whose family depends on his or her income should consider term life insurance equal to six to ten times gross pay. Another rule advises five times your gross income, plus such expenses as the mortgage, consumer debt, and kids' college costs. And the main rule of thumb is to buy only term life insurance instead of cash-value life insurance.

- Net worth. Net worth is the ultimate measure of financial success. It's all you own, minus all your owe. If you liquidated your life, what would you have left? For example, the equity you have in your home is part of what you own, while your remaining mortgage balance is what you owe. You own investments and belongings, while your car note and credit card balances are owed. According to the best-selling book *The Millionaire Next Door*, if you're interested in being a "wealth accumulator," your net worth should equal your age times your pretax income divided by 10. A 40-year-old with $100,000 in annual income should have $400,000 in net worth.

The main drawback for such rules of thumb is that spending should reflect your priorities. Some people would gladly buy an inexpensive car because cars don't matter to them. Perhaps they want to spend lavishly on gourmet foods, Christmas gifts, or electronics, because that's how they choose to spend money.

That's fine. But ballpark estimates can at least keep you in the ballgame.

Buying Tactics: When the Price Isn't Really the Price

Negotiating the best price on goods and services is standard practice in many countries, but Americans often don't try to haggle. As a result, many of us aren't very good at it and feel awkward asking for a better price.

But numerous face-to-face buying situations lend themselves to negotiation, outside the most obvious example of car buying. Big-ticket items, such as furniture and appliances may lend themselves to price negotiation. And you'll have better luck at privately owned retailers and service-providers than with national chains.

Here are some haggling tips:

- Develop a price plan. Entering negotiations without a plan can quickly lead to overpaying. First, you need to know a range of prices for the product or service. Then, decide on two price points, your ideal price and the price you could live with. The dollars in between are the negotiation battlefield. Also identify nonmonetary goals, such as getting the purchase completed quickly, service after the purchase, and maintaining a relationship with the seller. In beginning the negotiation, start with your numbers, not the salesperson's. Most important, maintain your walk-away power. If the salesperson won't negotiate within the boundaries you set, you need to walk away and reassess your price range or find another seller.

- Assess the balance of power. Evaluate how eager you are to buy, compared with how badly the vendor wants to sell. If you have more leverage—he wants to sell more than you want to buy—be aggressive. For example, you might be able to play hardball for a better deal at the end of the month if a salesman needs to reach a quota. On the other hand, if you want to buy a car with a six-month waiting list for delivery, the seller has more leverage. In that case, try to negotiate fringe issues that might not matter much to the seller. Haggle about better loan financing or get them to throw in floor mats. Leverage swings to you on multiple large purchases. If you're buying a room full of furniture rather than a single piece, the salesperson is likely to be more flexible on the total price.

- Seek win-win. If you will have an ongoing relationship with the seller, such as a private landscaper, housecleaner, or small-shop auto mechanic, it's often better to seek a deal that works well for both of you. That's not just to be nice, but because relationships can translate into saved dollars down the road. Where there's an element of trust involved, shoot for a fair price rather than the ultimate bargain.

- Know when to be ruthless. If many identical products are offered by lots of sellers with plenty of inventory available and no need for an ongoing relationship, it's take-no-prisoners time. Car buying might be an example if the same model car is available from a variety of sellers. You don't need a relationship with a private seller, a used-car lot, or even a dealership because you could get maintenance and repairs at any auto shop or another dealer. Your strength comes from your power to walk away and buy elsewhere.

- Be emotionless. Nothing zaps your bartering power more than being emotionally tied to buying. If a salesperson smells a hint of desperation, you're toast. Any leverage you had is gone.

- Request "best and final." Bids and offers are usually padded with room for negotiation. So simply ask for a best-and-final price, or ask, "Is that the best you can do on price?" If it's an in-person verbal exchange, remain silent and maintain eye contact until the salesperson responds. The silence is torture for some people, who will fill the void with an offer they didn't really want to make.

Will haggling work all the time? Of course not. It may not even work most of the time. But this is one case where the clichés apply: "It never hurts to ask," and "you won't get if you don't ask."

Curse of Automatic Payments: Monthly Commitments Will Haunt You

People save more money if they make it automatic. That's why it's so painless to save in a 401(k) retirement plan or a Christmas club account. You don't have to do anything. Automatic savings make people's lack of self-discipline work for them. This seemingly simple concept was the basis of a best-selling book, *The Automatic Millionaire,* by David Bach.

But the automatic approach has an evil flip side. It works against consumers when they're automatically spending instead of automatically saving. It's the health club membership you don't use anymore, the music club that sends CDs you don't want, the premium cable channels you don't watch, and the wireless phone minutes that go unused. The list of recurring monthly and annual charges goes on and on and amounts to a lot of wasted money. Check your bank statement or credit card bill for more examples.

Sometimes bad choices stem from good intentions. In the health club membership example, getting in shape is a good idea. If you use the gym several times a week, an annual membership ends up being cheaper than paying each time. But good intentions stray far from reality. Researchers found 85 percent of users who chose a monthly contract would have been better off paying by the visit. In fact, they were overpaying by an average of $700 during their membership term, compared with a per-use contract, according to research by Ulrike Malmendier of Stanford University and Stefano DellaVigna of the University of California at Berkeley.

Consumers generally don't work out at a gym as often as they anticipated when they signed up. The typical gym member used the facilities a paltry four times a month in the study.

So, automatic payments are most dangerous when we're making unsound judgments about ourselves, being too optimistic that we'll use the service that's incurring the regular monthly charges.

You can end the financial damage of automatic spending simply by canceling the products and services you don't need or use. Some commitments are more difficult to unwind, such as a vacation time-share, which can be notoriously difficult and expensive to unload. In that case the recurring payment is the financing of the timeshare, the maintenance fees of several hundred dollars a year, and the cost of traveling to the timeshare to use it.

To prevent automatic spending gaffes, here are some tips:

- Buy a la carte. Always prefer the pay-as-you-go option, at least at first, until you know how much you'll really use the service. In other words, be as afraid of spending commitments as a dedicated bachelor is of engagement rings. Avoid yearly contracts, even if they include a discount over the monthly rate. Most times, you can switch from month-to-month to a discounted annual rate after you determine whether the service is truly worthwhile.

- Don't forecast high use. Realize that the moment you make a purchase or sign a contract is the most motivated you may ever be to use that service. You can't count on that same level of interest in the future. In fact, choose the initial contract based on your worst future behavior. Then adjust the contract later, if you find you use the service more.

- Check the cancellation process. Many services with automatic payments make it difficult to cancel. A health club might only allow you to cancel in person. A credit card might require you to cancel by writing a letter. Those procedures are designed so you procrastinate the cancellation. If it's a cumbersome cancellation process, it might be a sign that you'll underuse the service.

- Tally the numbers. Most automatic payments are expressed as a monthly fee, because the dollars don't sound as expensive. A $25 monthly contract seems harmless enough. But multiply it by 12 and determine whether the service still seems worthwhile expressed as $300 a year.

If you could cancel or downgrade just four automatic contracts you don't use: a health club membership, $70 per month; a premium channel on the cable TV package, $15 per month; Internet access on your cell phone, $10 per month; and a movies-by-mail subscription, $18 per month. That alone would save you $1,356 a year.

That's how wasteful automatic spending adds up.

Buying Used: Secondhand Gives You a Leg Up

Buying used merchandise can end up being a good deal or a bad one by resulting in saved or wasted money. But being smart about buying previously owned items can be a key to spending smarter.

Nowadays, traditional outlets for used items, including garage sales, yard sales, flea markets, thrift stores, and newspaper classified ads, are augmented by such online options as auction site eBay and Craigslist.com.

Here are general criteria for evaluating whether to buy an item used instead of new:

- Savings. Buying used usually means taking on more risk because you can't return the item to a retailer or manufacturer. Therefore, the price difference between buying used and buying new must be large enough to compensate you for taking on this additional risk. Quickly depreciating items can be the best bargains. Their resale prices will be significantly lower soon after the initial purchase. Automobiles are the prime example. A car can lose 30 percent of its value in the first year. If you can swoop in at year No. 2 to buy a lightly used car and avoid the depreciation hit, you can save thousands of dollars. Timeshare vacations are another example. A new timeshare might cost $15,000, while buying from someone desperate to dump one could cost a small fraction of that.

- Buying used might or might not mean taking a step down in quality. For example, buying a used table made of real wood is actually superior in quality to a particle-board table purchased new. But if the item is lower in quality because it's been used, make sure the savings justify the downgrade in quality.

- Gross-out factor. Buying some used items might make you squeamish. Undergarments and mattresses are examples. Different people will draw the line at different types of purchases. Lingerie might be a definite no, while a secondhand pair of jeans might be okay. And you might evaluate shoes on a case-by-case basis. I didn't mind buying a used suit at a high-end consignment shop. I bought the suit for $24.99, along with two silk ties for $8 each. I've worn the suit at family functions and during television appearances. It fits great and looks great for a small fraction of what a new suit would have cost.

- Used quality. Some items are functionally no different used than new. Books, music CDs, video games, and some sports equipment, as long as they're not damaged, function the same way used as the day they were purchased new.

- Life span. Avoid items with short life spans. For example, an older model ink-jet printer might be cheap when purchased used, but you may no longer be able to find ink cartridges for it. Many items with rapidly evolving technology would fall into this category.

- Length of use. Ask yourself how long you're likely to use the item. The shorter the use, the better deal it is to buy used. Kids clothing is a great buy used because you know the child will outgrow the garment quickly. Kids toys can also be a good buy, considering many youngsters' short attention spans.

- Uncertainty of use. Avoid buying new if you're unsure about whether you'll get a lot of use from the item. If your child starts taking lessons on a musical instrument, it's best to buy a used violin or piano until you're certain he or she will continue for more than a few months. Consider buying used when taking up new hobbies, such as golf, skiing, or camping, that require expensive equipment. You can upgrade later, when you're ready to make a commitment to the activity. By then, you'll also be more knowledgeable about what type of equipment you'll need.

- Quality needed. Nobody needs top quality for every purchase. Storage shelving or bookshelves that will be out of sight in the basement can be purchased used, assuming the units are sturdy. If an item's aesthetic appeal is low on the list of priorities, it might be a good candidate for buying used.

- Complexity. The fewer moving parts, the better when buying used. In buying tools, a used hammer or wrench is low risk, whereas buying a used power saw is riskier. Exercise dumbbells are a better bet than a treadmill. Buying a used computer is a worse idea than buying a used patio set. An exception would be buying a complex item that is factory refurbished and comes with a warranty.

  Golf balls are pretty simple. That's why even though I'm an above-average golfer, I buy used balls. They're name-brand balls in mint condition. They play just as well—and hook and slice just as well—as new balls for a fraction of the price.

- Safety. Maintain a strong bias against used items that could be a hazard to adults and especially to children. For these items, price is less a concern than the quality of the item. If you have any doubt about the safety of a child's car seat or playpen, for example, consider buying new.

- Seller. If you know the seller, perhaps a relative, friend, or neighbor, you might have more confidence that the product has been well-maintained. That can give you peace of mind when buying it secondhand.

- Budget. Consider buying more items that are used if you're cash-strapped or trying to get out of debt. It can provide some breathing room for a tight household budget. And for a home business on a limited budget, buying used office furniture and equipment can help fatten the bottom line.

Saving money is the upside of buying used. Among the downsides are that shopping for used items often requires more time and effort than retail shopping, especially if done in person. And you're bound to end up with a defective item once in a while. Also, some people get sucked into the thrill of the bargain hunt and end up buying used items they don't need.

But if you can buy used items wisely, you'll often get good value for your money.

Spending Windfalls: Don't Blow It

We've all heard the stories about the lottery winners who go broke and the professional athletes and celebrity entertainers who go bankrupt. Blowing millions of dollars seems unfathomable, but it happens with disturbing regularity.

And multimillionaires aren't the only ones. Every day, regular people squander inheritances, court settlements, salary bonuses, tax refunds, and gambling winnings. That's because, contrary to popular belief, it's hard to spend money well. And wisely spending a windfall is even harder.

True, dealing with sudden money is a nice problem to have. But it's important to realize that windfalls, especially sizable ones, can be life altering. They potentially offer a more comfortable lifestyle or a path to self-destruction.

Up to 70 percent of people who receive large lump sums of money blow it in a few years, according to the National Endowment for Financial Education. So, the first rule of dealing with sudden money is not to lose it, which means maintaining as much respect for the money as if you earned it in a regular paycheck.

Here are other tips:

- Do nothing. Unless you're facing bankruptcy, don't spend the money for a while—at least three months and preferably six. During this period, don't dramatically alter your lifestyle. That means don't quit your job and don't start spending on luxuries. Park the money somewhere safe, such as a savings account or money market account. Growing the money isn't the first goal. Give yourself time to adjust to your new financial boundaries. And in the case of an inheritance from a loved one, you need time to grieve so confused emotions don't lead to bad spending decisions.

- Seek help. Develop relationships with professionals who can help you. Seek advice on such issues as insurance, tax planning, and estate planning. Some financial planners specialize in clients who become wealthy quickly, such as those found at www.suddenmoney.com. Be on guard for unscrupulous "professionals" who prey on those who suddenly come into large sums of money.

- Consider the wonderful possibilities. Play the daydream game everyone has tried. "If only I had more money, I could…" Besides home improvements and spending on luxuries, force yourself to add to the list meaningful and long-lasting uses, such as continuing your education, saving for retirement, or starting a business.

- Devise a plan. Tops on your spending list should be paying off debt, except possibly mortgage debt, and creating an emergency fund of three to six months of living expenses. Start or augment savings for such long-term spending goals as children's college costs and retirement.

- Enjoy it. Nobody needs to tell you how to spend money on fun. But start slowly and moderately. Before buying the red BMW 5 Series you always wanted, rent one for a few weeks to determine whether the thrill wears off and you would be just as happy with a slightly used Honda Accord. Before building an addition to your home, start with a smaller project, maybe with some interior painting. Before quitting your job and volunteering at a charity, work at the charity part time.

- Give. Sharing money, whether with family members or charities, brings a special joy—and possibly tax breaks. Favor giving over lending money, which often leads to headaches.

Whatever you do with your windfall, aim for maximum satisfaction and few regrets.

Membership Has Its Privileges: Savings by Association

"Membership has its privileges," says the American Express slogan. The ability to save money is among those privileges, not just for credit cards but many groups, clubs, and organizations.

The problem is, most people don't know about or use these lucrative benefits, which in essence they already paid for through membership fees or just belonging. That's why it's worth making time to learn about the side benefits of being a card-carrying member of groups you belong to. Examples are industry organizations and your local chamber of commerce. They're good for professional networking, but they might also offer access to group health insurance if you're self-employed. Your credit union or employer may have discounted tickets to amusement parks and concerts. Your mutual fund company might have useful financial planning tools on its Web site and offer a discount on tax-preparation software. Membership at a zoo in your hometown might provide free admittance to other zoos around the country.

Here are several common memberships and some of their lesser-known privileges. They could save you literally hundreds of dollars.

- AAA. This organization, formerly called the American Automobile Association, is known for its roadside assistance and towing service, hotel discounts, and free maps and travel guides. AAA has 49 million members in North America. But AAA has many other benefits too, including services to book your trip, not just plan it. The group has exclusive deals with Hertz rental cars and Disney amusement parks. Other perks are trip-specific.

For example, a member booking a cruise through AAA might receive a free cabin upgrade. AAA also offers favorable terms on credit cards, auto loans, money market accounts, and certificates of deposit. And it offers a variety of insurance, as well as advice and services for car buying. You can stop by any AAA branch office to obtain traveler's checks at no cost. Retail discounts include 30 percent off at LensCrafters eyewear, 20 percent off FTD flowers, and 10 percent off at Target and Payless ShoeSource. The AAA Web site (www.aaa.com) has an online tool for tracking maintenance on your family's vehicles.

I bought eyeglasses from LensCrafters, which were going to cost me a hefty $400. But after my AAA discount, the whole package of designer frames and lenses cost about $280. Granted, that's still a lot. But I paid a lot less than I could have for the exact glasses I wanted. My backup pair cost just $17 from an online retailer. And that included shipping and tinted clip-ons.

By the way, if you're a member of AAA, use its towing service and roadside assistance instead of one through your auto insurance. *Consumer Reports* found that using your insurer's service, even if the breakdown didn't involve an accident or traffic violation, could raise your insurance rates. You don't need both, so cancel your insurer's towing service.

- AARP. Formerly known as the American Association of Retired Persons, this group is the primary lobbying and information organization for people over age 50. AARP boasts 36 million members. Members receive *AARP The Magazine*, *AARP Bulletin*, and all the other benefits of membership, including discounts on insurance, as well as on travel and Internet access. More than 3,200 chapters offer driver safety courses and tax preparation help. One of the big AARP benefits is the Web site itself, at www.aarp.org, which is full of useful information. It also highlights discounts, such as 20 percent off at Reebok stores, 35 percent off AARP book titles through BarnesandNoble.com, and 4 percent off Home Depot gift cards bought through the AARP Web site.

- Warehouse clubs. Under such names as Costco Wholesale Corp., Sam's Club, and BJ's Wholesale Club, these stores offer wholesale-like prices on a variety of supermarket items and merchandise for the annual fee of about $50. But they offer other services too, including discount vacation packages, insurance, check printing, and film processing and photo printing. Some offer deeply discounted eyeglasses and prescription drugs, even diamond jewelry.

  BJ's, for example, offers discounted gasoline at the 88 service stations it operates. It offers home heating oil in eight northeastern states. It offers custom embroidery, custom-built sheds, and discounts on home-security systems. You can even use the club to buy a car for you with its auto-buying program.

- Credit cards. Most Americans have credit cards, but many don't realize all the fringe benefits they have. Many perks revolve around insurance for car rentals, travel cancellations, travel accidents, airline luggage losses, and hotel burglaries. When traveling abroad, paying by credit card is likely to yield a better currency exchange rate than cash or traveler's checks. Another common perk is an extended warranty on items purchased with the card. Check your agreement or call the customer phone number on the back of your card and ask what benefits you're eligible for.

  And that doesn't even include rewards cards, which pay you in cash, merchandise, airline miles, and other currencies just for using the cards. Unless it's a tremendous deal, stick with cash rewards cards. Of course, most all benefits of a credit card are wiped out if you regularly carry a balance and pay outrageous interest charges.

These are only a few examples of how membership has its privileges. The point is to get the most out of all your associations.

Shopping Online: Geek Your Way to Savings

Many smart shopping habits are rooted in common sense. They haven't changed much since your grandparents were young, or even their grandparents. But tools for being a smart shopper have changed dramatically in the past decade, with the dawn of widespread use of the Internet for commerce.

Shopping online, or at least researching a purchase online, has become fundamental to smarter spending. Here are a few reasons to incorporate the Internet into your shopping habits:

- Research. Nobody is knowledgeable about every product and service, so having the wealth of information available on the Internet is invaluable. You can search for products and read reviews. Amazon.com is especially good for looking up user reviews. Of course, Consumer Reports online, www.consumer-reports.org, is a standby of independent product tests, although you'll need a $26 annual subscription to see much of the content. ConsumerSearch.com compiles and rates product reviews, essentially providing a review of the reviews. A more informed consumer is always a better consumer.

- Price comparisons. You won't know what a good price is until you know what price different vendors are selling the item for. That type of comparison shopping used to be laborious. It meant traveling from store to store. Today, you can find competitive prices in just a few clicks of the computer mouse. You can search not only retail prices for new products but prices for used products too. Auction site eBay.com is the most obvious example of a site selling used items. To compare prices on new products, use a shopping robot, or shop-bot. Try such sites as Froogle.com, MySimon.com, Shopzilla.com, DealTime.com, and Shopping.com.

I used a shopping comparison site to upgrade my computer speakers. Speakers I liked at my local big-box electronics store, complete with a bass-booming subwoofer, cost $130. Too rich for my blood. I came home and ordered the same speakers on eBay for $29 plus $15 shipping, or $44. That still might seem excessive to some people, but it felt like a deal to me.

During a different electronics splurge for an audio receiver for my modest home theater setup, shopping online got me a $549 receiver for $318, shipped.

- E-mail newsletters. Visit your favorite retailers' Web sites and sign up to have their newsletters or sales fliers delivered by e-mail to your in-box. Some retailers offer subscribers good deals unavailable to the general public.

- Printable coupons. Some retailers provide coupons you can print out and bring with you to their bricks-and-mortar store. You can even print manufacturers' coupons for the supermarket. They're often more valuable than the coupons that come in the Sunday newspaper. Try such sites as Smart-Source.com, Boodle.com, Coupons.com, CoolSavings.com, and Eversave.com.

- Coupon codes. Called variously coupon codes, promotional codes, and discount codes, these codes are secret series of letters and/or numbers that during online checkout unlock such goodies as a percentage discount on your order, dollars off your purchase, and discounted or free shipping. Before making an online purchase, do a quick search for a coupon code. To find codes, use a regular search engine, such as google.com, or a coupon aggregator, such as CouponMom.com, Coupon-Cabin.com, FlamingoWorld.com, or CouponMountain.com. Codes are also found in retailers' newsletters and promotional e-mails.

- Rebate portals. While shopping on the Web, try entering retailers through the side door to discounts, called a rebate portal. A shopping portal, or entrance, is a separate free Web site that has an arrangement with retailers. Retailers pay a commission to portal operators for sending Internet consumer traffic to the retailer's site—a kind of referral fee. When the consumer makes a purchase, the retailer pays the portal a commission. A "rebate" shopping portal goes a step further and shares its commission with the consumer. It's akin to getting credit card rewards points or cash back for using a particular credit card.

For example, if you wanted to buy a $300 KitchenAid mixer at Cooking.com, you could go to a popular rebate Web site such as FatWallet.com and click on FatWallet's link for Cooking.com. That transports you to the retail site, where you shop as you would normally. But now, you'll get money deposited in cash in your FatWallet account. If the rebate is 6 percent, for example, two extra clicks to shop through the portal just earned you $18.

Heavy users of online sites could receive rebates of hundreds of dollars a year, especially if they're buying big-ticket items, such as computers and jewelry. Learn more about rebate portals at CompareRewards.com. When choosing a portal, give preference to ones that pay in cash, rather than points. Examples besides FatWallet.com are Ebates.com, Jellyfish.com, and QuickRewards.net.

- Sales tax. In many states, you're supposed to pay state sales tax on Internet purchases. But, as a practical matter, that rarely happens unless the retailer has a store in your state and is required to charge sales tax upon checkout. Otherwise, you can avoid state sales tax by shopping online. If you live in a state with 6 percent sales tax, that's $6 savings for every $100 spent. Of course, buying online often involves a shipping charge, which can offset any sales-tax savings.

- Hassle. You not only save money by shopping online, you can save time. What's easier than going online and making a purchase with a few clicks of the mouse? The item is delivered right to your door. A side benefit is that you avoid impulse buys that might tempt you in the mall.

If you're new to online shopping or wary about how safe it is, try a small purchase from a household-name retailer and see how it goes. You're likely to be pleasantly surprised. And you'll find that online shopping adds a valuable weapon to your arsenal as a smart consumer.

5

Around the House: Everyday Spending

Everyday spending is the prime culprit of needlessly wasting money. Some of the easiest spending cuts to make with the least pain will help you become financially FIT, as discussed in Chapter 1, "Financial FITness." Those areas are in food, insurance, and telecommunications, or FIT. However, other areas of daily spending are accomplices.

The common thread throughout this type of spending is that you pay over and over again, day after day, often without giving it much thought. Small one-time wastes of money aren't harmful, and frankly, aren't worth bothering about. But with repeated spending, even small savings grow in magnitude. They can be as expensive as the biggest one-time purchases you make all year.

Heating and cooling your home is a prime example. When it's cold, you need heat. When it's hot, you need air conditioning. For the most part, these are not optional. So, many people stop there, throwing up their hands and resigning themselves to paying the cost, whatever it is.

That's a mistake.

True, you have to pay for heating and cooling, but you can be smart about it and save a lot of money. The same is true for buying gasoline, cable TV service, or prescription drugs. Few people are able or willing to cut out these expenses altogether, but you can reduce them.

This chapter will help.

Running Hot and Cold: Keep Your Bought Air Indoors

It might not be surprising that you can save money on heating and cooling, or keeping your "bought air" inside your home. What might surprise you is learning the truth about the fantastically bad advice doled out by the media every summer and winter for cutting costs on heating and cooling. A surprising amount of the typical advice will actually cost you far more money than it saves. Fact is, some of the best steps you can take are cheap and free.

It's worth doing. The typical American household spends about $1,000 a year on heating and cooling, with heating accounting for about $800 of those on energy costs. Cutting that spending by a mild 10 percent yields savings of $100 just for one year. That's a decent savings but not huge, which highlights why you shouldn't spend a lot of money on energy-saving measures around the house.

There are only two main ways to save money on heating and cooling. You have to take steps that allow you to raise the thermostat in the summer and lower it in the winter. Or, keeping the thermostat the same, you need the furnace or other air temperature regulator to turn on less frequently, mostly by keeping your bought air indoors longer.

Those sound like ridiculously simple concepts, but they're important. They're important for all those people who in the dead of winter are walking around their homes in bare feet and a T-shirt. They're important for all those people who keep their windows closed and run their air conditioners when it's a beautifully breezy 70-degree day outdoors.

Because there's so much misinformation and confusion, below are clear do's and don'ts when it comes to cutting spending on home heating and cooling.

- Don't replace your windows. Replacing the current windows in your home with energy efficient ones to save money may be the worst advice ever spewed on the American public. Replacing windows is so expensive—easily costing thousands of dollars— that you'll be hard-pressed to ever make back in energy savings what you spent on the windows. It may literally take decades before you break-even and start saving even a dime. However, a completely different scenario is if you plan to replace your windows anyway, maybe for cosmetic reasons. In that case, it may well be worth getting more energy-efficient windows. It's much easier to make up in energy savings the price difference between two types of windows than it is between energy-efficient windows and not replacing windows at all.

- Do seal windows, doors, and cracks. To reduce heat loss through windows, repair broken ones and buy inexpensive, do-it-yourself window insulating kits at any hardware store or home center. The same goes for doors. Maybe even more important is to seal cracks, like those around pipe cutouts to the outdoors, gaps around chimneys, recessed lights, and unfinished spaces behind cupboards and closets. Seal them with inexpensive caulking and insulation. For more on sealing, see the publication "Guide to Energy Star Home Sealing" by the EPA. Call 888-782-7937 or get it online at EnergyStar.gov.

- Don't buy a programmable thermostat, necessarily. These thermostats by themselves do nothing to save you money. They're just timers to set the home's temperature automatically during certain times of the day and throughout the week. They are similar to a timer that automatically turns on a lamp while you're on vacation to deter burglars. If you're absentminded about turning down the heat when you leave for work in winter, for example, a programmable thermostat might help and could quickly pay for itself. But it won't make your furnace run more efficiently. In the old days, people accomplished much the same thing by walking over to the thermostat, raising their arm, and adjusting the thermostat by hand before they left home or went to bed. So, a programmable thermostat is mostly insurance against forgetting to set the temperature yourself—and a small luxury so you can wake up or come home to a house at a comfortable temperature. It won't help much if you have an erratic schedule and need heating and cooling at unpredictable times during each day. All that said, I installed a programmable thermostat in my home and find it useful, though not necessary.

- Do use free heating and cooling. Opening and closing blinds and drapes during the day can help control heat from the sun that enters the house. They also act as an insulator against drafts in winter or a shield against sun in summer. Open windows when it's comfortable outdoors. And don't forget the ultimate in free temperature control—the human body. Wearing a sweater and footwear in winter uses your free body heat to make you warmer. Dressing lighter around the house in summer allows you to raise the temperature and use less air conditioning. If you're insulted by how simple those suggestions are, reflect on times when you didn't dress appropriately for the weather and wasted energy.

- Don't heat with an open fireplace. Burning a wood fire in an open fireplace often sucks more heat from your home and shoots it up the chimney than it throws off in radiant heat. The effort or cost to acquire the firewood adds to the waste. However, using a wood-burning fireplace for ambience can be pleasant. Just realize you're actually paying to have the fire, and it's not a heat-source supplement. You can trim you energy losses by closing doors to the fireplace room and cracking a window an inch. That allows the fire to use oxygen from outdoor air instead of being fueled by your paid-for heated air. Lower the central heating thermostat to about 50 degrees while the fire is burning.

- Do vary the temperature. Somewhere the myth got started that it's cheaper to keep your heat or air conditioning on all the time rather than varying the temperature. It's not true for most heating systems, especially if you change the temperature by more than 5 degrees for several hours.

- Don't wildly crank the thermostat up or down. It won't heat or cool any quicker. You'll probably waste money because the system will actually cool the house more than you need—if you adjusted it to 50 degrees during a hot day, for example, when you really only needed it to be 72 degrees.

- Do seal ducts. Duct leaks account for 20% to 40% of energy loss, according to the Lawrence Berkeley National Laboratory, which studied the issue. But duct tape isn't the answer; it's actually a poor way of sealing duct cracks and seams. The best, but most expensive, way to seal ducts is have a contractor spray an aerosol-based polymer called Aeroseal through the ducts, which plugs the holes. That could cost hundreds of dollars, even a couple thousand. A cheaper idea is to use a mashed potato-like sealant called mastic. Use the water-based kind. You paint it on duct joints and tiny holes, and it hardens. Or use metallic duct tape with an UL-181 rating. Those do-it-yourself supplies cost a small fraction of professional duct sealing.

- Don't be careless about ceiling fans. Ceiling fans do nothing to cool a room, but they do create a wind chill that makes humans feel cooler. That simple fact has several implications. First, don't turn on fans in rooms where there are no people. It's a waste. But you can use fans and air conditioning together, as long as the fan's wind chill allows you to turn up the thermostat and use less air conditioning. In winter, common advice is to use ceiling fans to distribute warm air accumulated near the ceiling. That makes sense, but the truth is that modern well-insulated homes have relatively low ceilings where the temperature from floor to ceiling doesn't vary much. And if the fan creates that wind chill, you'll actually feel cooler and might have to use *more* heat. The federal EnergyStar program insists that if you use the ceiling fan's reverse setting to create an updraft, and you set the fan on low speed, air may distribute more evenly. You can try this, but remember it has to make your home so much warmer that you turn down the heat and save money. Otherwise, you'll be losing money because you'll be using the same amount of heat and paying for the cost to operate the fan. Speaking of fans, when the inside and outside temperatures are very different use kitchen, bath, and other ventilating fans sparingly. They can pull out a houseful of warmed air in just an hour.

- Do replace furnace air filters. Replacing filters monthly is standard advice. But the secret truth here is you don't need fancy air filters. The cheap ones at the home center that cost about 60 cents to $1 each work fine. Also, cover the filter slot with a piece of wide tape to make sure all the air goes through the filter.

Gasoline: Fuel Savings with Better Mileage

Rising gasoline prices irritate consumers more than the price of any other purchase. Maybe it's because we're reminded of the prices by gigantic signs as we drive through most every commercial intersection. If the price of milk was posted so prominently, perhaps we'd throw a fit when milk prices jumped a dime.

But there's good reason for consumers to pay attention to gasoline spending. The average household spends about $2,700 a year on gas. And while you have no control over gas prices, you do have control over how much gasoline you use. If you can improve your mileage just 20 percent, you could save hundreds of dollars.

The best way to save money on gas is to buy a higher mileage car, but that's only good advice if you're car shopping right now. Otherwise, here are some do's and don'ts to spend less on gasoline and squeeze more miles out of each gallon.

- Do check for the lowest prices in your area. Online site GasBuddy.com and others allow you to compare gas prices in your area as reported by fellow drivers. But don't go far out of your way to save a few pennies. Any savings will be used up traveling to a distant service station and back.

- Don't bother with gas additives. Advertisements for gasoline additives that supposedly deliver better mileage are exaggerations or outright lies, according to the Environmental Protection Agency, which has tested more than 100 of them. Some additives might even harm your vehicle.

- Do get a tune-up. A poorly tuned engine can increase fuel consumption 4 percent, and fixing a faulty oxygen sensor could improve mileage 40 percent.

- Don't be a lead foot. Each 5 miles per hour above 60 you drive is like paying an additional dime or more per gallon. Driving 75 mph, rather than 65 mph, could cut your fuel economy by 15 percent.

- Do replace air and oil filters. Clogged air filters can increase fuel consumption 10 percent.

- Don't drive like a jackrabbit. Anticipate traffic conditions to avoid sudden braking and acceleration. Aggressive driving can lower gas mileage 33 percent on the highway and 5 percent in the city.

- Do keep tires inflated. Underinflated tires can increase fuel consumption more than 3 percent. Find the proper inflation level on the driver's side door jamb or in the manual.

- Don't keep junk in the trunk. Each 100 pounds reduces gas mileage by 2 percent.

- Do use the right oil. Use the recommended grade of motor oil, preferably one with "energy conserving" on the label. Gas mileage could improve 1 percent to 2 percent.

- Don't piggyback. Carrying large items on the roof of the vehicle creates drag that can cut gas mileage 5 percent.

- Do use cruise control. Using your vehicle's overdrive gears and cruise control improves fuel economy.

- Don't overbuy. Buy regular-grade gasoline, unless your owner's manual says otherwise. Costlier high-octane gas does not improve performance and could actually hurt gas mileage.

- Do combine trips. Several short trips taken from a cold start can use twice as much fuel as one trip covering the same distance when the engine is warm.

- Don't run air conditioning unnecessarily, but don't lower your windows at high speeds, either. Both create drag on the car.
- Do take the smaller car on errands. If you own more than one vehicle, drive the one that gets better mileage for running around town.
- Don't idle. Sitting still yields 0 miles per gallon. The best way to warm up a vehicle is to drive it. More than 30 seconds of idling on winter days just wastes fuel.

More radical changes—albeit impractical for some people—include changing your work hours to avoid rush-hour traffic, using carpools and ride-sharing programs, taking public transportation, walking to work, and working from home.

Television: Tune In to Savings

Though many Americans would argue, pay television is optional entertainment. It's clearly a "want" instead of a "need," despite how some people may feel they "need" to watch a football game, a popular TV series, or even the nightly news.

On the other hand, TV can be relatively cheap entertainment, especially compared with such entertainment options as live events, sports activities, or many Americans' favorite entertainment choice, shopping.

But it's important not to overpay for television. Many families easily rack up $1,000 a year in television service and watch-at-home movies.

Today more than ever, Americans have alternatives to traditional cable-company TV service—alternatives that can save you money. For the first time, many Americans have choices among competing companies for receiving their TV signals, whether from satellite TV companies or traditional telephone companies. And the television set is not the only place to watch shows and movies anymore, with more people watching video entertainment on computers and handheld devices.

As with most products and services, the more competition, the better consumers fare on price and choices. The following are ideas for cutting your costs for video entertainment:

- View TV service as a luxury. If you're deeply in debt and have no savings, you can't afford TV service. That may seem harsh. But think about it in terms of dollars and time. First, you could redirect all those dollars spent on TV to better uses. Just as important, you could use those TV-watching hours to instead work and earn more, read a book or take a class to get a higher paying job, or do a household budget and financial planning. Once you're back on track financially, add subscription TV back into the household budget.

- Tier drop. Don't buy more service, or a higher "tier," than you need. Of the scores of channels fed into your home, how many do you actually watch? Research says the typical household regularly tunes in to 17 channels, while many TV packages deliver more than 100. And if you don't have a digital or high-definition TV, the digital tier might not do much for you. If you mostly watch news shows and game shows, as opposed to movies and sports, a better picture might be less important. And consider that to get the digital tier with a cable company, you also have to rent a converter box for every TV on which you want to receive digital channels. That adds to the overall cost. Check out the cheaper "family" tiers if you only subscribe to cable or satellite TV for the kids.

- Go online. Many TV networks allow you to watch their full-length programs free online. You can also buy and download your favorite shows a la carte to play on your computer or handheld device, such as a video iPod. Sports fans can see or hear many out-of-market games online, including Major League Baseball and even some college sports. Most people can rig a system to connect their computers to their televisions sets, if they want, although the picture quality might be inferior to regular TV. Meanwhile, some programs are available as free downloadable podcasts that you can play at your convenience.

However, some podcasts contain only the audio version of a program.

- Haggle. Call your service provider and tell them you want to cancel because it's too expensive. Listen to their offers to retain you as a customer. The representative may at least offer you a temporary deal, such as a reduced price for six months. You have more leverage if you have multiple services, a high bill, or competition in your area. Haggling won't work every time, but it's worth a few minutes on the phone to try. If you don't succeed at first, try again. Oddly, different customer service reps will often give you different answers and offers. And it's not unethical to ask for a discount. It's merely negotiating a price between two parties, something done in legitimate business every day.

- Buy bundles. Cable and phone service providers offer discounts when you subscribe to several services such as TV, Internet, and phone service in a bundle. Just make sure you actually need and want all the services in the bundle. Price out your options separately too, to ensure the bundle is actually saving you money.

- Examine premium channels. Instead of subscribing to premium channels, you could pay a la carte for movies. Do that by renting DVDs at a store or by mail service, such as Netflix and Blockbuster Total Access, which charge a monthly fee. Or watch pay-per-view movies from your cable or satellite provider. The exception is if you will definitely watch a lot of movies on the premium service every month. Find your break-even point. If Showtime costs an extra $20 a month but you can get pay-per-view movies for $4 each, you'll need to pay for five movies every month before Showtime becomes a better value, assuming you think the types of movies offered are similar.

- Subscribe seasonally. It's easier than ever to add and subtract services, such as premium channels. If you love an HBO series that only runs for six months, order only for those months and then cancel. Or if you watch a lot of movies in the summer while network shows are in repeats, subscribe to a premium channel just during the summer months. If you must have ESPN for college basketball, but don't like much else on ESPN or the tier that offers it, subscribe to the higher tier only during the season. Typically, there is no annual commitment for packages, giving you the flexibility to add and drop services to suit your seasonal viewing habits.

- Exploit the cable TV secrets. A little-known tactic for getting cheaper TV is to subscribe to the most basic tier, often less than $15 a month. It gives you all the broadcast network channels and a few others. Even less known is a federal law that gives consumers the right to purchase the cheapest cable tier and add premium channels such as HBO, Showtime, Cinemax, and Starz. It also allows lowest-tier subscribers to order pay-per-view movies. Most cable companies don't advertise these options, hoping you will assume you need a higher tier of service to have premium channels. Be aware, however, that the cable company can require you to rent a set-top box to receive premium channels or pay-per-view. The federal rules, called "tier buy-through" or "basic plus premium," do not apply to satellite TV.

- Compare satellite. Satellite television service has been an option for years. But the price savings with switching may be small depending on the package you order, and you'll need to install a satellite dish and buy a converter box for each television. Consumer satisfaction surveys have shown people are happier with satellite than cable service.

- Cut the cord. Cancel your subscription TV and go with what you can get free off the air, which now includes digital and HDTV programming. Your local electronics store can set you up with an antenna. Then, you can supplement broadcast offerings with DVD rentals of not only movies, but also previous TV seasons of shows. And don't forget your local library, which is a great source of free video entertainment. Meanwhile, non-TV entertainment can be found in such print sources as newspapers, magazines, and books, while other sources include radio and the Internet.

As more competition enters the TV service business, it will pay to keep an eye out for packages and services that are more appropriate for you than your current ones.

Pets: Don't Let Fido Sink Your Finances

America is largely a nation of pet lovers. That helps explain why in 2007 we spent an estimated $40.8 billion on our furry, feathered, and finned friends. For perspective, that's about the size of the entire economy of a medium-sized country, such as North Korea or Kenya, and more than Germany spends on its military. See Table 5.1 for how spending on pets has grown.

TABLE 5.1   Total U.S. Spending on Pets

Year	Spending in Billions of Dollars
2001	$28.5
2002	$29.5
2003	$32.4
2004	$34.4
2005	$36.3
2006	$38.5
2007	$40.8

Source: American Pet Products Manufacturers Association

But our love for animals doesn't quite explain Gucci brand "long-haired goat dog beds" for $2,050, sterling silver cat food bowls lined with yellow gold-plating for $1,220, Chanel Bow-wow perfume, caviar for cats, jeweled collars, monogrammed sweaters, and designer bird cages. And then there's pet Christmas gifts, doggie birthday parties, and, believe it or not, dog weddings.

It's important to realize that such lavish spending and pampering is solely to make the pet owner feel good. Because the truth is, the pet doesn't care. Most animals just require you meet their basic needs, such as food and shelter, while such social animals as dogs also crave human interaction. The overspending probably stems from a culture in which Americans show affection and appreciation through buying something.

But if the pet doesn't really appreciate what you bought, then it's a waste.

Following are the biggest categories of pet spending, how much Americans spent on them in 2007, and some cost-cutting tips:

- Pet food, $16.1 billion. Frugal consumers can check the Internet for pet-food recipes. For example, you can make dog food by mixing whole grains, oil, and chicken broth and baking it. Or you could shop for the best prices on prepared pet food and use coupons where you can. Warehouse clubs and discounters are good places to find inexpensive food. Although, some argue that if the food is inferior in nutrition, you could spend more on health care than you save on food.

- Veterinary care, $9.8 billion. Finding affordable health care for your pet is the same as for any purchase. Compare prices by calling local vets and asking for price quotes. Charges can vary widely. Although you may be comfortable with a particular vet, at least consider shopping around for a better price on routine procedures. And ask your vet to suggest inexpensive alternatives to pricey medications. However, most experts don't advise skimping on checkups and shots for pets that need them. A healthier pet will cost less in the long run. Pet insurance is a dicey topic but may not be worthwhile unless you have an old pet and can get relatively inexpensive insurance. Be aware of deductible amounts you have to pay and exclusions for what insurance will not cover. To gauge cost, the average annual surgical vet cost is $453 per dog and $363 per cat, although costs could run into the thousands of dollars. In the end, you might be better off self-insuring. You do that by saving in an interest-bearing account the money you would have paid in insurance premiums. Tap that account when your pet needs an expensive operation or treatment.

- Supplies/over-the-counter medicine, $9.9 billion. Prices for pet supplies can vary widely. Check the Internet for prices on medicines and dog grooming supplies, fish-tank filters, and cat-litter supplies. Prices can be dramatically cheaper, even with the shipping charge.

- Pet services, grooming, boarding, $2.9 billion. Professional grooming for a pet is similar to lawn care or housecleaning. You can save a bundle if you're willing to do it yourself. And getting a neighbor to watch a dog while you're on vacation is far cheaper than boarding, even if you bring the neighbor back a nice souvenir as a thank-you.

- Live animal purchases, $2.1 billion. Note that actually acquiring the pet is the least expensive part of pet ownership. Give greater consideration to the costs of care and feeding the animal. If you're looking for a cheaper but still enjoyable pet, consider colorful bettas, also called Siamese Fighting Fish. They're cheap, hearty, and low-maintenance. Birds, rodents, rabbits, and gerbils are also examples of relatively cheap pets. Owners tend to be less emotionally attached to those kinds of animals. And, as unpleasant as it is to think about, that makes it easier to let them die when they become injured or sick rather than spending a lot of money in a futile effort to make them well.

If you cut wasteful spending, your lower stress level from having less debt will be the greatest gift to your pet, giving Fido more joy than a $150 wall-mounted, ergonomically correct dog dish ever would.

Prescription Drugs: Just Say No to High Prices for Meds

The seemingly outrageous prices on name-brand prescription drugs aren't a surprise to most people who need the medications, but those people might not know they have cheaper alternatives.

That's important when drug prices and insurance copayments are consuming more of household budgets. Americans spent $250 billion on prescription drugs in 2006, according to the National Association of Chain Drug Stores. Medication expenses for individuals could easily run into thousands of dollars a year, depending on their prescription drug insurance plan—assuming they have one at all.

Here are ways to spend less money on prescription drugs. Any strategy you try should be cleared with your doctor.

- Substitute. Ask your doctor whether a less expensive medication would work just as well for your ailment. If you no longer need the power of a brand-name cholesterol-lowering drug such as Lipitor, for example, you may be able to switch to a less expensive name-brand drug or a generic drug, which is a copy of a name-brand drug. Generics, which despite the name are not inferior to name brands, can cost 20% to 80% less. On average, the cost of a brand-name prescription in 2006 was about $111, while generics cost about $32, according to the drugstore association. Generics are only available for drugs whose patent has expired. So, instead of thinking of generics as inferior to name brands, think of them as tried-and-true medications that have withstood the test of time. Insurance copays for generics often are less than for brand-name drugs.

  Another possible substitute for high-priced drugs is an over-the-counter medication—again, assuming your doctor approves. For those with insurance, you might find an over-the-counter substitute costs less than your prescription copay. For information on making cost-effective drug substitutions, go online to www.crbestbuydrugs.org for a Consumers Union report.

- Buy in batches. Most health plans through employers offer a mail-order option that allows you to buy drugs in larger quantities for a discount. A three-month supply by mail order can cost nearly the same as a one- or two-month supply at a retail drugstore. The savings on generics is even greater. When comparing prices of different quantities, convert prices to a price-per-pill by dividing the total price by the number of pills. The result will reveal the best deal. For those with prescription insurance, buying in larger quantities means shelling out fewer copays over the long run.

- Shop around. Drug costs can vary widely among pharmacies, so it pays to compare among online, mail order, and bricks-and-mortar retailers, especially if you take the medication regularly. Price comparisons and information are available at such Web sites as DestinationRx.com, PharmacyChecker.com, and

PillBot.com. Table 5.2 shows mail order, which includes online sales, is the fastest growing outlet for meds.

TABLE 5.2　We're Changing Where We Buy Prescription Drugs

Seller	Growth 2004-2006
Mail order	24%
Chain drug stores	14%
Mass merchants	13%
Independent pharmacies	8%
Supermarkets	7%

Source: National Association of Chain Drug Stores

- **Beware of free samples.** Free drug samples from your doctor sound like a good deal. But once the freebies run out and you have to fill the prescription, you could find those free medications to be quite costly. Some clinics and hospitals won't even use samples, claiming it's cheaper for patients in the long run to use generics than name-brand drugs that are prescribed just because the pharmaceutical salesperson gave the doctor samples.

- **Split pills.** One of the best ways to save money on drugs is to buy medications at double strength and split the pill in half. You take just half a pill to get the correct dosage. The bargain comes because often the price of medication is the same regardless of dosage. So, you end up paying half-price for the drugs or shelling out half as much in insurance copays. Pill-splitting is most precise when using a plastic pill-splitting tool, also called a tablet cutter, which you can buy at a drugstore for about $5. Be aware that some pills cannot be split, including time-release drugs and capsules. And the patient must be able, physically and mentally, to split pills and be dedicated to doing it.

- **Canada conundrum.** Buying brand-name drugs from Canada can be cheaper, but it's technically illegal. *Consumer Reports* recommends that if you are determined to buy a name-brand drug from Canada, go to PharmacyChecker.com for a list of approved outlets and look for the seal of approval by the

Canadian International Pharmacy Association. Generic drugs are more likely to be cheaper in the United States.

- Get aid. People without insurance or with low incomes may qualify for a variety of programs that help pay for prescription drugs. Among them, according to Consumer Reports Money Adviser, are Partnership for Prescription Assistance (www.pparx.org); Rx Outreach (www.rxoutreach.com); TogetherRxAccess (www.togetherrxaccess.com); along with federal, state, and local government programs.

Library: Free Stuff Galore

One of the worst ways to waste money is to voluntarily pay for things you can get for free. And few places offer more free stuff than your local public library.

Of course, it's not really free. But you will pay for the library with your tax dollars whether you use it or not. So you might as well get a library card and check out the surprising array of offerings at one of the 16,000 public libraries in the United States.

Here's a sampling of the offerings at libraries:

- Reading materials. Books, magazines, newspapers, and printed research and reference materials are standard fare at libraries. They might not offer the same ambience as sipping a $5 coffee at a retail bookstore, but at least you can leave with your reading material—free. Even in rural locales, libraries are likely to have a robust assortment of fiction and nonfiction books and the latest subscriptions to popular periodicals. The average family of four spends $136 a year on reading, according to federal government estimates. Surely, some of that spending on reading could be substituted free by going to the library occasionally. And the benefit multiplies if you use the consumer advice books and magazines to help spend your money smarter.

- Internet access. Free online access has become a standard service at virtually all libraries. And today, a quarter of public libraries and two of three academic libraries offer wireless access, which means you can bring a wireless-enabled laptop computer and log on free. If you're a light Internet user, perhaps checking e-mail a few times a week or doing occasional Web searches, canceling your home Internet service could be worthwhile, especially if a library is nearby. If your high-speed Internet access costs about $40 a month, that's a savings of nearly $500 a year. Libraries also offer access to expensive online databases of information.

- Entertainment. For adults, eight of ten libraries offer cultural programs, including talks by authors and musical and theatrical performances. Occasionally swapping in a cultural program at the library instead of two tickets to a show could save hundreds of dollars a year. For the kids, libraries may offer such fare as story hours, puppet shows, and skits.

- Business resources. Libraries offer business resource centers with information on how to start a small business, find a job, or write a good cover letter. Some offer seminar series or network and mentoring programs.

- Recorded music. Most libraries carry an extensive collection of audio CDs. It could pay to listen to an artist first before wasting money on a CD you don't enjoy.

- Videos. Most libraries now carry a lot of mainstream movies, not just how-to and documentary videos. And many offer the video in DVD format, not just VHS tapes. Most families could easily cut in half their monthly video store spending by swapping in one or two older movies from the library. And borrowing children's videos is perfect for children who want to watch a program several times but then grow tired of it.

- Recorded books. Books on tape or CDs are great for long car rides, airport layovers, or exercising, but they're expensive. Libraries lend audio books at no cost. Some libraries even offer digital MP3 versions of audio books, letting you download them to your own computer or handheld device. There are no late fees because the books "time out" at the end of the lending period, and you just delete them.

- Meeting rooms. Reserve free space at the library for meetings and community gatherings, a service that might otherwise cost hundreds of dollars.
- Instructional programs. Libraries offer free classes, including programs on identity theft, how to buy or sell a home, gardening, or using common computer software, such as Microsoft's PowerPoint.
- Research. Research librarians are among the most helpful people you'll ever meet. Most are pros at using both printed research books and expensive electronic databases that you'll have free access to.

To locate a library near you, consult your phone book or check an online list at www.publiclibraries.com.

Compact Fluorescents: See the Light

Savings opportunities at home are all around us, including the nearest light fixture. That fixture and many like it around your home are probably excellent candidates for compact fluorescent lamps, or *CFLs*.

Using compact fluorescent bulbs saves you money, both on the bulbs and on electricity costs. In fact, each bulb will save you at least $30 over its life compared with incandescent bulbs, according to conservative estimates by the Department of Energy.

It's a savings that adds up fast once you start counting the number of light bulbs in your home. But it's a tough choice to make because it first appears that CFLs are more expensive, because you pay more initially for a single bulb. Maybe that's why CFLs only make up about 5 percent of the light bulb market, according to energy department estimates.

The bottom line is that consumers are actually wasting money by purchasing traditional incandescent bulbs for all their fixtures.

In fact, it can pay to remove perfectly good incandescent bulbs and replace them with CFLs. While there are many environmental reasons for trying CFLs, there are also financial ones. Here is generally what you need to know about compact fluorescents:

- Price. Every product that runs on energy has two prices, the upfront purchase price and the operating cost. CFLs are cheaper on both counts. CFLs last 8 to 15 times longer than incandescents. So, although it's true that one CFL might cost $3.50 and one regular bulb is 50 cents, you would have to buy maybe a dozen bulbs at a total cost of $6 before one CFL goes dark. So, over time, CFLs win on initial purchase price.

  Second, through its life the CFL uses a quarter of the electricity of a traditional bulb. If bulbs were cars, that's like replacing a car that gets 20 miles per gallon with one that gets 80 miles per gallon.

  So, using the energy department's estimate of $30 savings per bulb, which is conservative, replacing just 25 bulbs reaps $750 over the life of those bulbs and probably much more.

- Quality. Years ago, the high cost and lower quality of CFLs discouraged consumers. The bulbs didn't turn on right away, and when they did, they flickered and hummed while giving off an unappealing color. And they were too large for many fixtures. Overall, it was an expensive, inferior product. But in recent years, the cost of CFLs has plummeted. Today, they are smaller and better quality. If you tried them before and were dissatisfied, it's time to try them again.

- Other benefits. Because CFLs last so long, you'll have to replace them less often. That means less hassle trying to regularly change bulbs in hard-to-reach places, including ceiling fans and outdoor fixtures. Another benefit is that because CFLs have such low wattage, you can produce a much stronger light in the same fixture. And CFLs stay cool, which can cut air-conditioning costs in the summer. They also come with long warranties, often five years or more.

- Drawbacks. You probably can't use regular CFLs in every fixture in your house, including those on dimmer switches. You can pay a premium for dimmable CFLs, but you might be dissatisfied. For example, dimmable CFLs have a narrower range of dimming and might be unsuitable for a very dimly lit home theater. There's no problem with three-way CFLs, except they're a little more expensive.

Also, many CFLs have a slight, but perceptible, delay in coming on and becoming fully bright. You might find that either annoying because it's different or enjoyable because it's less abrupt than an incandescent's instant-on. Read product packaging for other restrictions. You might have to try a few brands before you get one you like.

Be aware that CFLs contain a tiny amount of mercury, though hundreds of times less than thermostats or old-style thermometers. For that reason it's best not to dispose of CFLs in the household trash if better options exist. Find out your disposal options at www.earth911.org or by calling 1-877-EARTH911.

- How to buy. At a savings of more than $30 per bulb, consumers might be tempted to run out and buy CFLs for all their fixtures. But start with replacing your five most-used bulbs. By easing into CFLs, you can get a sense of the differences, while still saving money. The bulb size might be slightly different and the shape will definitely be different, with many looking like an ice cream cone spiral.

Buy bulbs by brightness, called *lumens*, instead of wattage. For example, a traditional 60-watt bulb and a 15-watt CFL both produce about 800 lumens. See Table 5.3 for a conversion chart.

TABLE 5.3   Light Output Equivalency

Incandescent Wattage	Lumens	CFL Wattage
40	450	9-13
60	800	13-15
75	1,100	18-25
100	1,600	23-30
150	2,600	30-52

Source: Energy Star

The packaging of many CFLs prominently displays its incandescent equivalent. Also, note the color, measured in "degrees

Kelvin." If you want a similar light color as many incandescent bulbs, look for CFLs with the color temperature of 2,700 degrees Kelvin or labeled "warm white," which has a yellowish hue. The color at 3,000 will be neutral white, while those over 4,000 will be bluish-white, or "daylight."

Buy only Energy Star rated CFLs, and look for good deals on them in multipacks in home centers and warehouse clubs.

To research more on CFLs, start with an online guide by advocacy group Environmental Defense at www.environmentaldefense.org/go/cflguide. The guide, which includes reviews by people who used the bulbs, asks where you'll use the bulb and what shape it is, along with any special features you want, such as being dimmable. It then suggests appropriate brands and model numbers of CFLs. The Energy Star CFL Web site, www.energystar.gov/cfls, has a product search section, along with other information.

Keep receipts from purchases of CFLs. They have long warranties. If one doesn't last as long as it should, you can have it replaced with proof of purchase.

Lawn and Garden: Grow Your Savings

Some 85 million U.S. households, or three out of every four, does some sort of gardening and lawn care, according to the National Gardening Association. Those households each spend an average of about $400 a year on plants, power equipment, fertilizer, and other products and services that comprise the $34.1 billion lawn and garden industry.

So examining your lawn and garden spending is worthwhile. Here are tips to help you get the most bang for your green-thumb buck:

- DIY. The most obvious way to save money is to do it yourself, if you are able, instead of hiring a landscaper to mow the lawn, mulch and weed the flower beds, and perform other chores. Time is the trade-off for many people who contend they are too busy to attend to landscaping.

But you should ask yourself whether you are really too busy to carve out an hour a week to mow the lawn, for example. At a mowing charge of $35 a week for six months, you could save more than $840. Exercise in the yard might even allow you to cancel your health club membership, which saves hundreds of dollars more.

However, if yard work makes you miserable and you have the money, paying for help might be money well spent. You must decide its value.

- Lawn. There are three simple rules for cutting grass, but many homeowners don't follow them. They are to set your mower deck at its highest setting, don't cut more than a third of the grass height, and leave grass clippings on the lawn. Not only will these tips help make your lawn look lush, they will save money by allowing you to use less fertilizer and weed killer. Grass clippings provide essential nutrients for the soil, and longer grass can choke out weeds before they grow.

  Contrary to popular belief, leaving clippings on the lawn does not cause a buildup of thatch. Thatch is caused by overfertilizing, so save money by not adding extra fertilizer. Overfertilizing also causes more hassle because the grass grows faster, and you'll have to cut it more often.

- Weeds. Prepared weed killer in a bottle can be expensive, especially compared with cheaper alternatives. For killing weeds in sidewalks and patios, douse them with boiling water or vinegar. You can save money on vinegar by diluting it with water, using just one part vinegar to two or three parts water.

- Tools. Gardening experts advise buying good-quality gardening hand tools rather than cheaper ones likely to break within a single season. But you don't have to buy them new. Check yard sales, especially of older people who might be selling quality tools made decades ago. If you have a small garden, skip power tools. Use hand tools, which are less expensive and will probably save time because you don't have to deal with electrical cords or fuel.

  When you do have to use gardening power equipment, such as a tiller or lawn aerator, coordinate with neighbors and rent equipment for the day, taking turns using it. It's not only cheaper but avoids the hassle of storing a large, seldom-used piece of equipment.

- Composting. Homemade compost can be better fertilizer than anything you buy in a store, and it's free. You don't need a fancy compost bin; just a 3-foot-square space. Pile on your yard waste, egg shells, coffee grounds, and pretty much anything that was alive but not part of an animal. The pile will start to stink if you use animal remains.

  The drawback of composting is it's a slow process. You will have to wait about nine months to start using a passive compost pile. But if you are more conscientious about mixing materials carefully, such as balancing vegetable waste with leaves, and rotating it to allow in air, you can have good compost in three months.

  The composting process highlights a general point about frugal gardening: You can save money if you're willing to wait. Buying smaller plants, such as trees and shrubs, is cheaper but requires patience before they become the size you envision.

- Mulch for less. Dyed hardwood mulch for garden beds is not only expensive but soon fades to the color of undyed mulch. So you're paying extra for a temporary appearance. Mulch also could be as simple as shredded leaves saved from the fall. You can shred leaves by running over them with a lawn mower. Straw is also a cheap alternative to wood mulch, and stone is more expensive initially but less costly over the long term because you won't need to replace it.

- Share. Swap cuttings and divisions of plants with friends, relatives, and neighbors. It's a free way to introduce new plants into your gardens. Local nature preserves and botanical gardens often host plant sales and sell their plant divisions inexpensively.

- Water. One way to save money on your water bill is to attach a barrel to your home's downspout to catch rainwater. Ideally, the barrel would have a spigot for easy access to the water, but filling watering cans works too. Use soaker hoses where you can. It is the most efficient way to deliver water to your plant roots and wastes less water.

And, in general, water gardens deeply but infrequently. Light daily sprinklings are a bad idea because they encourage shallow roots in plants, which in turn require more frequent watering.

- Vegetables. At first, growing vegetables won't be cheaper than buying them at a supermarket because of startup costs with a garden. But over time, vegetable gardening can end up being less expensive. Even if gardening turns out to be about the same price as supermarket produce, gardening can be a good value because you're getting superior quality.

Eyeglasses and Contact Lenses: See the Price Difference

Prescription eyeglasses and contact lenses are part of everyday life for many people, yet the vast majority are wildly overpaying for their corrective eyewear.

Americans spend $28.7 billion annually on vision products and services, according to the Vision Council of America. Eyeglass frames and lenses make up the largest portion, about $16 billion. While you probably can receive slightly better prices on contact lenses, eyeglasses are the bigger opportunity for huge savings.

Still, many of the 147 million adult eyeglass wearers probably don't know that because few shop around. Prices vary widely. People can pay more than $1,000 for a pair of glasses, while at least one Internet provider promises a pair for $8. An identical pair of eyeglasses—same lenses and same brand of frame—costs from $178 to $390, depending on the optician or optometrist, according to research in seven U.S. cities by Consumers' Checkbook, a consumer information guide.

The single most important consumer tip for buying eyeglasses or contacts is to relax. Inexpensive glasses pose no health risk to your eyes. Even a bad pair of glasses won't give you an eye infection or permanently damage your eyes, although they could cause headaches until they are fixed. And once a doctor fits you for a particular brand and type of contact lens, you can buy them anywhere and they should be identical to what your doctor sells.

So you should consider comparison shopping. In fact, a 1978 Federal Trade Commission ruling, called the Ophthalmic Practices Rules, says you have a right to take your prescription anywhere to buy glasses. A similar law for contact lenses exists, called the Fairness to Contact Lens Consumers Act, passed in 2004. It dictates that your eye doctor must automatically give you your prescription after he fits you for contact lenses. Doctors can't charge for it or make you sign a waiver.

The point of these mandates is to break the domination of eye-care practitioners selling corrective lenses. That's where prices are likely to be highest. To be fair, though, people report receiving the best service from their neighborhood optician or medical-center eye doctor, according to a survey of 92,000 readers of Consumer Reports magazine.

The decision about buying glasses and contacts generally comes down to where you buy them. The simpler your prescription, with normal measurements and no bifocals and trifocals, the better luck you're likely to have buying from a cheaper source than your eye doctor.

Here are categories of eyewear outlets, with tips for buying glasses.

- Doctors and independents. If you're willing to pay more for glasses in return for good service, buy from your eye doctor or an independent optical shop. Buying eyewear could include a trust factor that might be higher with your doctor or a neighborhood optician.

  They are also likely to carry brand-name frames, which is largely a personal fashion choice. But the secret about name-brand frames is companies such as Giorgio Armani and Ralph Lauren don't make the frames, Consumer Reports said. They just license their names to a regular frame manufacturer. So you might find a very similar and cheaper frame made by the same manufacturer that doesn't bear a designer name.

- Chain stores. If you're willing to pay to get your glasses quickly, try a chain store, such as LensCrafters, which promises glasses in about an hour. Be sure to receive the discounts you're eligible for. For example, a discount with a AAA membership might be more valuable than using your employer vision insurance. Be aware the person you talk to at the chain store is mostly a salesperson whose job is not only to help you, but help you spend the most money.

- Warehouse clubs. If price is important, try a warehouse club. Costco Wholesale Corporation scored very high with Consumer Reports readers and Consumers' Checkbook findings. BJ's Optical, found in Eastern states, also scored well. For some warehouse clubs, you don't need a membership to buy glasses.

- Online. If price is paramount, try an Internet merchant. I bought prescription glasses from Zenni Optical, www.zennioptical.com, for $8 and am pleased with them. With shipping and an optional clip-on sun shade, my total bill was $16.90. But there are other online glasses retailers. Reviews of them are available at EyeglassRetailerReviews.com and GlassyEyes.blogspot.com.

One advantage of ultracheap glasses is that, even if everything goes badly with your transaction, you're not out a lot of money. That makes online retailers an ideal outlet for buying a backup pair of eyeglasses. Of course, you won't have an optician to adjust the frames so they're comfortable and to ensure bifocals are aligned properly with your eyes.

You could also try a hybrid plan, where you buy frames online and take them to an optician to have lenses inserted. You'll have to judge whether the hassle is worth the savings.

No matter where you buy eyeglasses, view lens add-ons skeptically. You'll be offered a variety of lens materials and coatings, such as polycarbonate lenses or anti-reflective coating or polished edges. For add-ons that you can test out, ask to see samples of glasses with and without the feature to determine whether it's worthwhile.

With contact lenses, the best tip is to get advice from your eye doctor about the different types of lenses, get a trial pair with a fitting check-up and perhaps even buy the first set from the doctor. But afterward, buy lenses—especially disposables—elsewhere, such as a warehouse club, by mail order, or on the Internet. Lenses will be identical to what your doctor can get, so there's no advantage to paying more. Savings with contact lenses won't be as large as with glasses, maybe $50 to $100 each year.

The big idea is to shop for corrective lenses somewhere besides your eye doctor to see your way clear to savings.

Clothing: Better Duds for Less

Clothing is a necessity, but spending a lot of money on it isn't. Apparel expenses are low-hanging fruit to cut spending from a household budget. It's easy to save, look great and still wear name brands, if you know how.

A family of four spends an average of $2,850 a year on apparel and apparel services, according to the federal government's Consumer Expenditure Survey. That's nearly $240 a month. So it is an expense worth addressing. Here are ways to do just that:

- Do nothing. Most adults have enough clothes to get by for months. If you need to get out of debt or save money quickly, make do with what you have. That may seem obvious, but it helps to acknowledge consciously that you don't "need" new clothes right now.
- Buy used. This is the crux of saving big on clothing—buying high-quality, name-brand used clothes. If you refuse to buy secondhand, you will not save much on clothes in the long-term. To buy quality clothing inexpensively, you'll need to get acquainted with secondhand stores, such as thrift stores and consignment shops. The scene is not usually the stinky, disorganized store with rumpled clothes that you might envision.

Many of today's secondhand stores are more akin to regular retail stores. Many of the clothes are just lightly worn. Some are new, with original tags. Of course, as with any used purchase, secondhand clothing must be examined thoroughly for flaws. For example, don't forget to test zippers.

Buying used clothes for children can save even more because kids outgrow garments so quickly. Besides the obvious idea of hand-me-downs from siblings—or even other relatives, friends and neighbors—try online auctions, such as eBay, which can be a good source of kids clothing bargains.

If you're uncomfortable buying used clothes, take baby steps by buying one item, maybe something inexpensive at a high-end consignment shop. I've had good luck buying a suit, a tuxedo, and neckties at a secondhand store.

- Use garage sales wisely. Garage sales can be sources of great bargains. But for adult clothes, it's more like a time-consuming treasure hunt than shopping for what you need. Chances are low that you will happen to find great clothes in your taste, your size and in a color that looks good on you during the few minutes that you happen to show up at the sale. Your chances improve when there is more inventory in one place, such as at a church rummage sale.

However, garage sales are a tremendous outlet for children's clothes. That's because you can buy items in a child's current size or future size, knowing they will grow into the clothes. And for younger children, style and colors matter less.

- Strategize. Many adults assemble their wardrobes haphazardly, buying items that strike their fancy. Instead, organize your closet and take inventory of what you have. That way, you can determine what you need. Write it down. Also, reflect on the colors and styles that look good on you. And, buy for the size you are now, not the size you someday hope to be.

For children, hold a fashion show with them periodically to determine what still fits, what doesn't and what's too tattered. That planning will allow you to take an organized approach to shopping.

- Simplify. Buy classic styles that will look good for years. And assemble a base of neutral colors—blacks, khaki, navy blue—that can mix and match to create a number of outfits. The same concept goes for shoes.

- Save on buying retail. If you won't buy secondhand clothes, go to your favorite store's Web site to check its sales every week. Similarly, sign up for your favorite store's e-mail newsletters to receive coupons and learn about coming sales. If you can't wait until the end-of-season sales to save money, at least wait until mid-season.

  And take a quick tour through such discounters as T.J. Maxx, Target and Wal-Mart to see what type of clothing you would be willing to buy at those places. Realize that inexpensive clothing likely to last only a single season—or maybe two—ends up being expensive for adults, compared with quality clothes that could last much longer. But discounters are a good deal for children' clothes.

- Maintenance. Realize that garments that must be dry-cleaned cost more over their life. Also, be wary of fabrics that tend to pill or wear too fast. And put your clothes in the dryer for just a few minutes, then hang them to dry.

6

Financial Foolishness: Overspending for Financial Services

The financial services industry is fueled in great part by money that consumers simply do not have to spend. That's a bold statement, but it's true. Banks, investment firms, and a myriad of other financial institutions thrive in part because consumers are intimidated by the world of money and are ignorant about how it works. Consumers' dollars leak through carefully planned cracks in the financial system, like a dripping faucet that ends up wasting hundreds of gallons of water.

We have talked about why many insurances are unnecessary and how much money consumers waste on insurance. But the waste doesn't stop there. Consumers are unnecessarily paying fees for simple bank accounts, paying far more than they need to for the privilege of having a credit card, and throwing money away by chasing hot mutual funds that will almost certainly underperform the market.

The good news is the financial services world is full of noise you can tune out—daily movements of financial markets and ridiculously complicated financial products, for example. It all amounts to a lot of blah-blah-blah that shouldn't affect your money life in the least.

This is purposefully not a book about investing, so we won't cover all the types of investment vehicles, such as Roth Individual Retirement Accounts (IRAs) and Exchange Traded Funds (ETFs). But following are just a few topics on how to spend your money smarter on financial services.

Bank Accounts: Don't Pay Anyone to Hold Your Money

Where competition thrives, consumers win. The banking industry has more competition than ever with the introduction of online banks. So, you don't have to put up with overpaying for checking and savings accounts.

The main idea is to remember that you're giving them the privilege of holding your money, so it's up to the bank to sell itself to you.

Still, banks today are nickel-and-diming their customers with ever-increasing fees. The average ATM fee is $1.64, with 98.3 percent of all banks charging such a fee, according to a survey by Bankrate.com. Table 6.1 shows how ATM fees have risen. If you want interest on your checking account, you might have to shell out an average of about $11 per month and maintain a balance of $615, on average. The average bounced check fee is more than $27.

TABLE 6.1   ATM Fees Rising

Year	Fee
1998	$0.89
1999	$1.12
2000	$1.33
2001	$1.36
2002	$1.38
2003	$1.40
2004	$1.37
2005	$1.54
2006	$1.64

Source: Bankrate.com

All those fees could easily devour any meager interest you earn on checking and savings accounts. They could essentially force you to pay the bank for using your own money, a losing proposition.

Here are tips to avoid unnecessary bank fees:

- Shop around. You want a bank account that fits your needs and doesn't charge fees. For example, if you work in a job that pays in tips, you may need unlimited access to tellers to sort through your deposits of bills and coins. But if you do your banking online and at ATMs, investigate what perks a bank will give you for forgoing teller visits, an expensive service for banks to provide.
- Find free checking. There are enough competing banks that you should insist on free checking, with unlimited check writing, no minimum balances, and no monthly service fees, whether a flat fee or based on the number of checks you write. Even better is an interest-bearing checking account. But if you keep getting zapped with low-balance fees, shift money into a free checking account. The scant interest the accounts pay isn't worth even a few low-balance penalties.
- Order your own checks. Of course, free checking isn't free because you have to buy the checks. But you don't have to buy them from your bank for up to $25 per box. Other companies will print checks at a fraction of the price, often $6 to $8 for a box of 200 checks. They work just as well. Check out deals from Wal-Mart, www.walmartchecks.com, for example. For more choices in background designs, search the Internet for "check printing" and find such sites as www.checksinthemail.com, www.checkworks.com, and www.checksunlimited.com.
- Use combined accounts. Sometimes you can avoid minimum-balance rules if you have multiple accounts or loans through the same bank. Also, some banks will base the minimum on the combined balances of all your accounts.
- Try online banks. You don't get to make small talk with a bank teller, but banking online is a better deal for most people because the minimum balances needed to avoid fees are lower. Also, online banks' interest-bearing checking accounts yield significantly more than bricks-and-mortar banks on average.

That means you're achieving investing's Holy Grail, greater return for no more risk, assuming the online bank is federally insured (FDIC). For savings, try such online banks as Emigrant Direct, www.emigrantdirect.com; ING Direct, www.ingdirect.com; and HSBC Direct, www.hsbcdirect.com. All offer far more interest than traditional savings accounts. If you're uncomfortable with online banking, try opening an online account with a small deposit until you become more comfortable with the process.

- Use automatic transactions. Online bill paying and automatic bank account withdrawals can eliminate the expense of a check. It also ensures you don't get hit with late fees. For example, you might allow the electric company to automatically debit your checking account to pay your bill. In addition, automatic deposit of your paycheck gets money into your account quickly and efficiently, which may prevent overdraft penalties.

- Try your credit union. Credit unions have a long tradition of offering some of the most consumer-friendly bank accounts. They're worth a look.

- ATM fees. Americans waste billions of dollars a year taking withdrawals from another bank's teller machine. The most obvious advice is to manage your cash, so you can always take out fee-free money from your own bank's ATM or one affiliated with your bank's ATM network. Failing that, if a grocery store is nearby, buy something small and pay for it with a debit card. Then get cash back by charging more than the amount of the purchase. You won't have to pay a fee, and the result is the same as an ATM withdrawal. Fortunately, some banks are eliminating ATM fees altogether as a marketing tactic, but it's not yet widespread.

- Beware overdraft loans. When a bank customer's account is empty, the bank will cover a check, ATM withdrawal, or debit card transaction without warning or notice. Then when the customer makes a deposit, the bank takes back the overdrawn money plus a fee of, say, $20 to $35. Worse, it's a "service" the customer never requested, but some banks automatically attach it to accounts. Many consumers would be better off if the bank just rejected the withdrawal request when there was not enough money in the account. Though not technically loans, the fees can be equivalent to a loan with 1,000 percent interest. So it's worth taking great pains to make sure you don't overdraw your accounts by diligently monitoring them and maintaining a cash cushion.

Credit Cards: Play the Game Right

Credit card companies are masters at separating you from your money. But you have power too. For example, did you know credit-card companies will take a little less money from you—and all you have to do is ask? You just have to know how to play the game.

A secret of the credit card industry is this: If you've been a long-time customer and have paid on time, a card issuer will bend over backward to keep you—even if it makes less money. That's because it's cheaper for card issuers to cut you a break than lose your business and have to find a new customer, which involves marketing and other expenses.

Periodically, you want to call your card company and ask for three things: a lower interest rate, a higher limit, and waived fees. You can save literally thousands of dollars.

So you don't get tripped up in trying to land a great deal, use the following script when calling your credit card company—and do it today. The script is adapted from a variety of sources, including a free e-book "Credit Card Insider Tips" by Cindy Morus.

Call the phone number on the back of the credit card and prepare yourself to be polite but aggressive during the conversation. Remember, you won't be hurting anybody's feelings by making these requests. And each time you call back, you're likely to get a different operator who might give you a better deal.

Here are the three requests you should make:

- Lower my interest rate. The less interest you pay, the more you can put toward eliminating the debt completely. A script might go like this:

  You: "Hi, can you tell me what my current interest rate is?"

  Operator: "Your current interest rate is X percent."

  You: "Hmmm. I would like you to lower my interest rate now, please." Don't say another word. The ball is in their court, and they'll fill the silence with an offer.

  Operator: "Okay, I can lower it to X percent."

  You: "That's not enough, but I will take that for now. Thank you for your help. I'd like to tell your supervisor how helpful you've been. Could you pass me over?"

  Supervisor: "How can I help you?"

  You: "First, I wanted to let you know how helpful the operator was. She/he did an excellent job of helping me. Now, can you tell me what my interest rate is?"

  Repeat script above. Then, call back in a month or two and do it all again. Don't worry about nagging them. It won't hurt your relationship with a giant card company, and you might luck into a new deal it is offering. The point of asking for a supervisor is that he or she may be authorized to do more for you than the operator is.

- Raise my credit limit. This one is a little trickier and seems counterintuitive. You might wonder why you'd want more credit available if you're trying to get out of debt. The reason is your credit score, which is partly calculated on how much debt you have compared with your available credit. So, even if your credit card balance is always $1,000, it's better to have a limit of $5,000 than $2,000 because you're using less of your total available credit. That can help your credit score, which can, in turn, help you qualify for lower interest rates on a mortgage or car loan, and even lower insurance rates. So it translates to real dollars.

  But your credit score might fall if the credit card company makes an official inquiry to your credit report—or "pulls" a report—and denies your request for a higher limit. So use the same basic script as given in the previous example, except when asking for a higher limit be sure to ask, "How much can you raise my limit without pulling my credit score?" Here too, you can double-dip by asking for a supervisor.

Another advantage to having a higher limit is avoiding an over-the-limit fee, which happens when you max out your card. You're less likely to do that with a higher limit. Be aware that the danger of having more available credit is that you could spend more and incur even more debt. If you know yourself well enough to realize that's a danger—you always end up maxing out your cards—then skip this request.

- Cancel my card fees. With competition among cards so fierce, there's often no reason to pay an annual fee. Ask the operator to waive the fee. When you get that, ask the operator to waive the current year's fee that you already paid. If just one card company eliminates its $50 fee for the current year and next year, that's $100 you made in about two minutes. A bigger issue is why you even have a card that charges an annual fee. Many do not, and it might be worth switching.

Similarly, if you were late with a payment but otherwise have a good payment history, call and ask for the late fee to be waived.

Of course, these scripts won't work all the time, and conversations are likely to deviate from the scripts. Just roll with it. If your efforts fail, ask the supervisor what steps you should take to get a lower rate, raised limit, or canceled fee. And realize these tactics work with such large companies as Visa and MasterCard but rarely work with department store charge cards.

Although getting better terms on your credit cards is a great idea, it doesn't fix the fundamental problem if you're in debt. If you carry a balance, you spent more money than you could pay. No amount of haggling with card issuers will fix that. You need to know why your spending exceeded your ability to pay. When the smoke clears, there are only two possible reasons: You spent too much or you didn't earn enough. So, those are the issues to deal with in the long term.

In the short term, try to get better terms on your credit cards. You're not guaranteed to win the game, but if you don't ask, you're guaranteed to lose.

Credit Cards II: Advanced Tactics

Credit cards are clearly a vice for many Americans. They're an easy way to overspend and buy stuff you can't afford. Even people who don't carry a balance are likely to spend more using a credit card than cash, studies show.

But for all their ills, credit cards can have advantages for some consumers, namely people who can control their spending. Realizing there are many ways credit cards can hurt your finances, here are some of the ways they could help:

- Built-in benefits. The first benefit of using a credit card and paying off the balance is improving your credit score, or FICO score, which allows you to spend less on interest for other borrowing, such as house and car loans, and even insurance. Other benefits of using a credit card are lesser known. They might include a host of insurances, including car rental insurance, travel cancellation insurance, travel accident insurance, airline luggage insurance, and hotel burglary insurance. You're likely to get favorable foreign exchange rates for using a credit card overseas.

  For purchases, some cards will replace or repair merchandise you buy with the card if the item is defective, stolen, or destroyed. Others will automatically extend the manufacturer's warranty. Other cards offer such perks as concierge services, upgraded hotel rooms, peak-demand restaurant reservations, or free valet parking.

  And you are not liable if the card is stolen and fraudulently used. But to use the benefits of your card, you'll have to take the time to learn about them. Go online to the credit card Web site or call the number on the card to inquire about the card's benefits.

- Rewards. Getting something for nothing is the ultimate in smart spending. And that more-or-less describes rewards credit cards. You can reap a host of freebies, from cash and merchandise to gasoline and airline miles. A rewards card credits you with points for every dollar you spend on your credit card. Then you redeem your points for cash or free stuff. The danger comes if you use the rewards card to spend more money than you would otherwise. And for those who carry credit card balances, rewards could be dwarfed by the extra interest you would pay with a high-rate rewards card. In choosing a rewards card, find out how quickly you can accumulate points and ask yourself whether you really want the stuff you get with points. In general, give preference to cash rewards cards, which are simpler and often more lucrative than earning points to spend on merchandise or airline tickets. In looking for a rewards card, try these Web sites: CardRatings.com, CardWeb.com, Credit-Reviews.com, Bankrate.com, and CreditCards.com.

- Risky tactics. With all the competition among cards, some people are tempted to game the system using dangerous tactics. One is "surfing" balances from one 0 percent introductory offer to another. Continually transferring your debt can reduce the amount of interest you pay, but it takes diligence. The danger of surfing arises when you make a late payment or let the introductory period expire without surfing to another card. In both cases, the card company will raise the interest rate, maybe to more than 20 percent. The same is true if you exceed the credit limit on the card. And many transfers involve a balance transfer fee that eats into your savings. If lack of discipline is the reason you're in credit card debt in the first place, you'll probably fail at card surfing.

Debt Reduction: Finish Paying for Your Purchases

One of the smartest ways to spend your money is to get out of debt. Whether you carry a balance on credit cards, borrowed money against your house, or financed your car, you probably have debt.

Carrying a reasonable home mortgage is acceptable, but most other debt is probably standing between you and wealth. Americans have $2.16 trillion in nonmortgage debt, according to the Federal Reserve Bank. That averages $7,250 for every person in the country, children included.

Here are ideas on getting out of debt and spending your paying-off-debt dollars wisely.

- **Don't shuffle debt.** Lots of advice is doled out about debt strategies. But much of it simply moves your debt. Examples are using debt consolidation services, wrapping debts into a refinancing of your home, or surfing your credit card balances to a lower interest-rate card. The objective is not to get the lowest interest rate on your debt. It's to get rid of it—fast. Choosing the best place for your debt is like choosing running shoes for a marathon. It matters, but it won't determine whether you win.

- **Address the problem.** The only reason for debt is that you bought something you didn't pay for. Either you overspent or your income wasn't big enough to cover necessities. Whatever the case, debt is only the symptom. Try to fix the root problem, whether spending or income. A temporary fix, such as consolidating credit card debt into a house refinancing, will clear your card balances. But unless you fixed the root problem, those balances will build again.

- **Use windfalls.** It's easy to see how spending money on eliminating debt is smart. Say you have a typical federal tax refund of $2,700. You have a choice of paying credit card debt, saving the money, or buying a fancy television. Which would you choose? The result after one year is that $2,700 turns into $3,186 by paying off an 18 percent credit card, because you'd avoid paying $486 in interest. You'd earn $81 in a 3 percent savings account. Or that $2,700 turns into about $1,350 if you bought a TV, and a year later it's worth about half what you paid. So your tax refund can earn you $486 or $81, or lose you $1,350. The choice is clear. Pay the debt.

- **Pay more than the minimum.** Try cutting spending and put that toward debt. Just an extra $100 a month can make a shocking difference. An $8,000 balance on a 14 percent credit card with a minimum payment of $172 would take almost 30 years to pay off, and you'll pay $9,100 in interest, according to a calculator at Bankrate.com. If you added $100 a month to the initial minimum payment and used that amount each month, you'd pay it off in three years and pay about $1,850 in interest. See Table 6.2 for details.

Thirty years or three years. Which would you choose?

TABLE 6.2 Pay the Minimum on $8,000 Credit Card at 14% Interest

	Payment	Interest Paid	Years to Pay Off
Minimum payment (initially $172.40)	$172.40	$9,104	29.5
Initial minimum, plus $100	$272.40	$1,852	3.1

- Focus efforts. Pay minimums on all your debts except the one you've decided to attack. So, for example, that would mean putting an extra $100 per month toward your targeted debt, rather than paying an extra $20 on five different debts.

- Snowball the payments. When you complete one debt, add that entire monthly payment to the payment on your next debt and so on. Each time, you're putting more money toward debts as you proceed through them. Debt reduction grows and accelerates like a snowball rolling downhill.

- Choose a pay-down strategy. Which nonmortgage debt should you pay off first? After paying for basic necessities and the minimums on all your consumer debts, extra money can go toward debt in three ways.

You could pay the loans with the highest interest rates first. Simple math tells you this is a wise choice, and it's the most commonly advocated method. That's because you'll end up paying less interest by attacking loans that cost you the most money. For example, paying off a $3,000 balance on a 14 percent credit card saves you $420 a year, while paying $3,000 toward a student loan at 4 percent saves $120. The disadvantage is your highest rate debt might also be your largest, so you could be stuck paying the first debt for a long time and feel like you're not completing anything.

Or you could pay the smallest debt first. This method disregards math and goes straight to human behavior. If you pay your smallest debts first, you'll eliminate several of them quickly and get a sense of accomplishment. It's like losing a few pounds the first week you're on a diet. It's an encouragement to keep going. Paying the smallest debt first also reduces the number of creditors on your mind. It's easier to feel in control of three debts, rather than 12. The disadvantage is you could pay more interest in the process—especially if you're not focused and the debt lingers for years. But if you are serious, the satisfaction of crossing debts off the list could result in more commitment and paying debts quicker, which means paying less interest.

Or you could use a hybrid method. You could combine the preceding two strategies by knocking out the smallest debts first—say, all those less than $1,000—and then paying the big ones in order of interest rate, highest to lowest.

But remember, the strategy you choose is less important than resolving to rid your life of consumer debt and then doing it.

Index Mutual Funds: You Can't Beat 'em, So Join 'em

Investing in stock mutual funds can be complicated, but it doesn't need to be. If you want to spend your investment dollars wisely, buy low-cost index funds.

Stock mutual funds, a collection of stocks in a variety of companies, are a great way to invest for the long term, meaning five years or more. But how do you choose among the thousands of funds operated by brilliant Wall Street money managers?

The short answer is, you don't. You buy index funds. It's the best way to spend your investment dollars.

In any purchase, whether an automobile or a pair of jeans, consumers make buying decisions using certain criteria. They at least want decent quality at a fair price. But a smart shopper's dream is to find above-average quality at a below-average price.

That adequately describes a stock index mutual fund, which mimics an established benchmark, such as the Standard & Poor's 500 stock index. The main alternative to buying an index fund is to buy a more expensive actively managed fund. Managed stock funds are operated by professional money managers who try to pick winning stocks. Winning is typically defined as beating the established index.

Stop and think about that. You're paying professionals extra money in the form of higher fund fees, and all they have to do is beat a mindless index that does nothing. That's not an accomplishment. That's the least they could do for their pay. But most fail.

That sets up the long-running philosophical argument between stock-pickers and indexers. And it's no wonder consumers are confused. Evidence supports the counterintuitive ideas that doing nothing is better than doing something, and you don't get what you pay for—both of which are rarely true in other parts of our lives.

In fact, many money managers must be losers because in the financial markets for every buy, there's a sell. A manager can only make you money if someone else loses money. The markets are a zero-sum game.

In 2006, 76 percent of active funds investing in large U.S. companies failed to beat a large-company stock index benchmark, the MSCI U.S. Prime Market 750, according to data from Morningstar, Inc. For large value funds, which try to pick undervalued stocks, 94 percent of active funds failed to beat the value index. And 2006 was not an unusual year. Failing to regularly beat the markets is a pattern active funds repeat over and over. As a group, they are consistent losers.

Yet investors continue to trust their hard-earned money to stock-pickers in the vain hope of beating the market. Here are reasons to buy index funds, based on criteria consumers would typically use for any purchase:

- Quality. It's extraordinary and newsworthy when a stock-picker can outperform an index over time. In fact, they only need to beat the market for a few years to become wildly famous. That means index funds are high quality because most actively managed funds can't beat them consistently. In many years, index funds beat about three-quarters of actively managed funds. And if you pick a fund that outperforms the index one year, it frequently has a hard time repeating that the following year.

- Price. Index funds are cheaper than actively managed funds because you don't have to pay a stock-picker. And index funds don't buy and sell stocks as frequently as managed funds, so the transaction costs—the costs to buy and sell stocks—and tax effects are likely to be much lower. A key reason index funds are high quality is because they are cheap, which means they return more of the gain to the investor.

- Warranty. An index fund won't protect you from general market downturns, but you won't see years where your fund does terribly compared with the benchmark index. You're also protected against bad stock-pickers who stray from the types of stock you want to own. So, like the factory warranty on a refrigerator, you're protected from something unusually bad happening. You will get what you paid for at a fair price.

- Cost of ownership. A higher-cost managed fund isn't a one-time expense. You'll pay higher costs year after year due to the built-in expenses of the fund. It's like buying what you think is a nice car. But you know it will be expensive to operate, maybe needing frequent repairs and getting lousy gas mileage, compared with other cars.

- Ease and convenience of use. The iPod digital music player is popular because it's easy to use. So are index funds. You could buy a single mutual fund that will give you the aggregate returns of all U.S. stocks, for example. If you want to invest in the stock of foreign companies, you can buy an international index fund. Actively managed funds are more complicated—not more sophisticated and superior, just more complicated.

You can use index funds to assemble most any portfolio you want. For example, a 40-year-old might assemble a retirement portfolio of 60 percent in a broad U.S. stock index fund, 20 percent in a broad foreign-stock index fund, and 20 percent in a bond index fund. Most mutual fund families offer index funds, including especially good ones at Vanguard, Fidelity, and T. Rowe Price.

Even with these no-brainer reasons for choosing index funds, investors will continue to chase "hot" mutual funds in hopes of beating the market. But the truth is, you can't beat 'em. So you might as well join 'em by using index funds.

Identity Theft: What Protections are Worthwhile?

Consumers are scared into spending money unnecessarily every day. Among the newest boogeymen is identity theft.

That's not to suggest identity theft isn't a serious problem for some people. And part of being a smart consumer is protecting your personal information so it's not misused. But the attention identity theft receives seems overblown: Just 1.5 percent of Americans annually are victims of thieves opening accounts fraudulently, according to a report by the Federal Trade Commission.

Fear generated by incessant discussion of identity theft, however, can make people susceptible to sales pitches for ID theft products and services. Many are not worth buying. In fact, some come-ons could be attempts to steal your identity, further victimizing the victim.

The truth is, identity theft often does not cost consumers a lot of money, at least directly. Federal and state laws limit a consumer's liability for whatever a thief does with your identity. For consumers who discover the identity theft within five months, two-thirds have no out-of-pocket expense, according to a study by the FTC. The most serious

and relatively rare type of ID theft—opening new credit accounts—
cost consumers an average of $1,180, most of it in cleanup costs.

Of course, when banks and other companies absorb the cost of
theft, consumers ultimately pay in the form of passed-along higher
prices. Perhaps the bigger cost is the hassle of cleaning up after ID
theft, which on average took 30 hours, the FTC found. Other estimates are far higher.

The biggest problem with ID-theft statistics is what's included.
Misuse of a credit card number counts as identity theft. In fact, it's by
far the largest form of identity theft. But consumers are protected
from fraudulent charges on their credit cards. It's no-cost, because
most card companies won't hold you liable even for the federal limit
of $50 per card. And resolving the problem is relatively low-hassle.
Just phone your card company and dispute the charges. It will issue
you a new card.

This is exactly what I did when someone stole my American
Express card number and began charging things at Blockbuster's
video-rental site online. I called to report the fraudulent charges.
Amex sent me a new card, which arrived a few days later, and it elim-
inated the charges from my bill. It was low hassle, compared with all
the nightmare stories you hear.

Adding to consumers' fear is the perception that ID theft is usually perpetrated by some anonymous criminal mastermind who has
chosen to become your evil twin and rip you off. The fact is, more
than half of serious ID thefts are perpetrated by people the victim
knows.

All this is to say you should be knowledgeable and guarded about
identity theft, but you shouldn't be scared into buying bad products
and services.

Here are do's and don'ts for protecting your identity:

- Don't buy identity-theft insurance. While cheap, many experts say this is not worthwhile. Insurance, which costs roughly $2 to $15 a month, covers some incidental costs of cleaning up a case of identity theft. It includes such reimbursements as mailing costs, phone calls, and lost wages, which doesn't help people on a salary. Some might cover pre-approved attorney fees. But most victims of ID theft incur few, if any, out-of-pocket expenses and won't collect anything from insurance. Many policies have a several-hundred-dollar deductible—a portion you pay before insurance kicks in—that will exceed the costs of cleaning up the mess.

  Perhaps the biggest problem with ID theft insurance is that people misunderstand it. They think that if, for example, someone steals money from their bank or investment account, the insurance company will repay them. Not so: Insurance won't pay for stolen money. So, while $25,000 in ID theft coverage sounds like a lot of protection for a small premium, policies are so limited that you're extremely unlikely to recoup anything near that much. Consumer Reports and the Privacy Rights Clearinghouse are just two of the expert sources advising against buying ID theft insurance.

- Don't necessarily pay for a credit-monitoring service. Credit monitoring doesn't prevent the crime of someone applying for credit in your name. It just alerts you that something already has happened. Monitoring services typically cost $50 to $155 per year, with $12.95 a month as a common price. But monitoring your credit reports is something you can do yourself for free by looking at your credit report. See details next.

- Don't buy credit reports. You no longer have to buy credit reports. You can receive them free from the three credit bureaus once a year at www.annualcreditreport.com, which is the only official site to provide free reports. It's safe to type in your Social Security number to the site. The first time you check reports, you should check all three credit bureaus, Equifax, TransUnion and Experian, although all three often have the same information. A year after your initial check, stagger your reviews by checking one report every four months. If you haven't examined your credit reports for errors and fraud—and for everyone in your family—do it today.

Note that while you don't have to pay for a copy of your credit report, you do have to pay to see your three-digit credit score, which determines how credit-worthy you are. You can get it online at www.myfico.com.

- Don't necessarily buy a credit restoration service. This is something you could do yourself, though it can be time-consuming. If your identity is stolen, restoration services—sometimes available through insurance policies—promise to help you clean up the mess and reclaim your identity. But realize that a restoration service can't necessarily do everything for you. Many creditors will only deal with you, not a third-party service, unless you sign over power of attorney to the restorer.

- Don't buy credit-card insurance. If you're not liable for fraudulent charges on your credit card—and, you're not—what are you insuring against?

- Don't use personal checks. Avoid writing checks, which have a lot of personal information on them. Checks might include your name, address, phone number, bank name, bank account number, electronic routing number and signature. It might also include your driver's license number, which in some states is your Social Security number, if the store clerk wrote it on the check.

- Do guard your information. An easy, free way to limit your chances of getting your identity stolen is to safeguard your personal information. You also should review your financial statements regularly and carefully. The quicker you catch identity theft, the less likely you'll incur a major hassle or expense.

- Do buy a shredder. Micro-cut shredders, which turn paper into tiny chips that can't be reassembled, are ideal. That is opposed to a ribbon shredder that cuts in strips. As a general rule, the smaller the confetti a shredder makes, the better. In short, shred anything that has your Social Security number on it or any account number.

- Do be smart about mail. Opt out of credit card offers at 888-5OPTOUT or OptOutPrescreen.com. This will prevent a thief from stealing a card offer from your mailbox and signing up for a card. Don't put outgoing mail with identity information on it in your mailbox, where a thief could steal it. And consider buying a locking mailbox.

- Do consider placing fraud alerts on your credit report. Paid services, such as the heavily advertised "LifeLock" service, place a fraud alert on your credit report for 90 days. That means whenever anybody tries to apply for credit in your name, the bank or creditor will see the alert and will likely take extra precautions to confirm your identity. These paid services renew the fraud alert when it automatically expires every 90 days. But you can renew a fraud alert yourself, if you're willing to contact a credit bureau every three months. You only need to contact one bureau to place an alert. It will notify the others.

  Beware that whether you do it yourself or pay for a service, fraud alerts are a potential hassle because you might not be able to apply for credit on the spot—for buying a car, getting a mortgage, applying for a charge card or activating a wireless phone contract, for example. You could speed the double-checking process by providing your cell-phone number as the contact number to confirm your identity.

  Whenever you activate a fraud alert, you're eligible to receive another credit report from each of the bureaus. So instead of receiving three free reports a year, you could get 15—your regular three free ones, plus three others every 90 days.

  With an alert, potential lenders can still access your credit report, but they will see a note that a fraud alert has been placed on the report.

- Do use a credit freeze if you're very worried about ID theft. A credit freeze is more restrictive than a fraud alert. You can freeze your report, meaning lenders can't access your report until you provide a personal identification number to temporarily lift the freeze.

  You don't need to renew the freeze every 90 days, but most people have to pay a fee, usually $10 to each of the three bureaus, to activate and lift credit freezes. So initially freezing all three reports might cost $30. ID-theft victims and people over age 65 frequently are exempt from the fee. You must contact each bureau separately, perhaps in writing by certified mail, which adds a minor expense. Rules and fees are first dictated by state law and then by the credit bureaus for states without their own credit freeze laws.

To find out more about your state's law and how to freeze your credit, go to FinancialPrivacyNow.org, a Web site of Consumers Union. But like a fraud alert, you won't be able to receive instant credit, and potential employers will be unable to perform a background check until you lift the freeze. It could take several business days to have a freeze lifted.

- Do use credit cards. Ideally, you want to expose someone else's money to the risk of your daily transactions, and not your own. That's what credit cards provide, as opposed to personal checks or debit cards. You often are not liable for fraudulent charges made with a credit card, and at most could be out the federal limit of $50 per card.

Debit cards are an alternative. But it's easier to dispute a credit card charge and not have to pay it, rather than persuading a bank to put stolen money back into your account after a debit card theft. You could be waiting for weeks while the bank investigates.

But using credit cards is a dangerous strategy for those who carry a balance subject to hefty interest charges. In that case, you'd be better off using cash.

In sum, the only spending you must do to protect yourself from identity theft is to buy a shredder and potentially pay credit freeze fees. All other purchases are either highly optional or a waste of money.

So, if ID theft typically doesn't cost consumers much money, why does the FTC receive more complaints about it than any other type of fraud? It probably stems from an emotional issue. Victims feel violated, similar to having their home broken into and ransacked, even though nothing was stolen. They get very upset, not at losing money but that someone would rob their most personal asset—who they are.

7

That Time of Year: Seasonal Strategies for Spending Smart

Every year, expenses arise that can pinch the household budget. But the truth is, some of them are annual events that you could, and should, plan for.

Is it a surprise that the kids need new school clothes in August and September? Did you not foresee Valentine's Day? If you've spent money on Christmas gifts every year of your adult life, did you think this year would be different?

If you don't foresee and plan for seasonal changes in your job, you could be fired. Why would you operate your personal finances so haphazardly?

We often overspend for annual events because we don't plan for them. First, we don't save money for the expense—in which case the purchase ends up on a credit card to potentially rack up interest charges. Second, we spend too much because we ran short on time and rushed into bad buying decisions.

This isn't rocket science. Skip a half-hour TV show one night, and you'll have time to plan for the next seasonal expense.

Back to School Spending: School Daze

Everybody knows holiday spending and the annual vacation will be big-ticket expenses throughout the year. But back-to-school shopping seems to sneak up on many families. And, in fact, some families might spend more money on getting kids ready to go back to school—especially if college students are involved—than any other spending event of the year.

Back-to-school shopping is different than it was a generation ago. Purchases stretch beyond No. 2 pencils, a lunchbox, and a pair of jeans. For some students, calculators, personal digital assistants, cell phones, and backpacks on wheels are standard gear. Trendy clothing and shoes can wipe out a school-shopping budget in a single lap around the mall.

American families with school-age children spend an average of $563 on back-to-school shopping, according to the National Retail Federation. Nationwide, it's an $18.4 billion shopping spree.

To cut the waste in back-to-school spending, consider these strategies:

- Plan and budget. Those words elicit yawns, but they're fundamental to using money wisely. School shopping shouldn't begin at the mall. It should start with a conversation. Plan with your children what you must purchase and how much it's likely to cost. That means taking an inventory to determine what supplies and clothing are missing and creating a shopping list. It also means forecasting what expenses are likely to crop up during the school year, such as new cleats for baseball or soccer, spending money for a school trip, or cash for prom or a yearbook. Be clear about how much money you, as a parent, will contribute and what extras must come from the child's own spending money. That should prompt a discussion of the difference between "needs" and "wants." Gym shoes are a need; $150 gym shoes are a want.

- Start early. Start back-to-school shopping closer to the Fourth of July than Labor Day. See Table 7.1 for when people say they begin shopping. Get a list of specific school supplies your child needs. Find out if the school or parents organization offers a school-supplies bundle. With bulk buying, it's likely to be cheaper and definitely will be less time consuming than trudging to a store and hunting for just the right color folders and brand of glue. For college students, starting early gives you time to search for used textbooks online or order international editions of texts, which tend to be cheaper but contain the same material.

TABLE 7.1   When Will You Begin Shopping for Back-to-School Merchandise?

At least two months before school starts	15%
Three weeks to a month before	45%
One to two weeks before	32%
The week school starts	5%
After school starts	3%

National Retail Federation, 2007

- Hold a fashion show. Determine what's missing from each child's wardrobe or what's too small or tattered to wear for the next school year. Create a list of items to buy, and budget a specific dollar amount for each child. With teens, set a dollar amount and give them some discretion over what they buy. Explain the concept of trade-offs—buying expensive soccer cleats means buying just two pair of jeans rather than three. Of course, mom and dad retain veto power over any purchases.

- Buy short-term items used. Some clothing and school supplies are used for such a relatively short time that they're hardly worth buying new. Ask friends and family for hand-me-downs, or host a neighborhood clothing-swap party. Check out thrift stores for bargains. With younger students, don't call them used or hand-me-downs. Instead, call them "first-grade clothes," as in, "You get to wear these special clothes when you graduate to first grade." Backpacks and scientific calculators are items to hunt for at yard sales or online auctions, such as eBay. If the student needs a computer, consider one with lower specifications. You don't need top-of-the-line computer power to run word-processing programs. If the child wants a high-powered gaming machine, require him or her to pay the price difference.

- Compare. Use the usual savings tactic of comparing prices. Backpacks can cost $10 or $40, and school scissors can cost 50 cents or $3. Personal digital assistants and computers may be cheaper at online retailers. Visit a warehouse club, such as Sam's Club, BJ's Wholesale, or Costco for bargains on clothing and school supplies. Dollar stores are good sources of off-brand items, such as tape and glue. And even if your teenage child refuses to buy clothes in a discount store such as Target or Wal-Mart, they might not mind buying such items as underwear and socks there.

- Buy late. An alternative to early shopping is late shopping. Limit clothes buying until after school starts, which allows you to spread out the expense over the year. And inevitably, your son or daughter will return to school and discover some new fashion he or she simply must have. Buying during prime time in August can be a good plan if you can find true bargains at back-to-school sales, and if your state holds a sales tax-free shopping event in August.

- Spend cash. Avoid using credit cards if you'll carry a balance from month to month. And if teens are doing their own shopping, give them cash too. Tell them as long as they get everything on their list, they can keep the leftover money. Then you'll see some smart spending.

Holiday Spending: Ho, Ho, Ho. Where'd My Money Go?

Holiday spending can have its own momentum, like a snowball rolling downhill. The result is not only overbuying on gifts and holiday-related merchandise but making purchases unrelated to Christmas, Hanukkah, and other late-year celebrations.

Many Americans return from the mall to spill out their largess from colorful shopping bags, only to realize some items aren't for gift recipients at all. Americans fork over an average of nearly $800 on holiday merchandise, according to the National Retail Federation. They will spend an additional $100 on themselves, the survey showed.

There are some obvious reasons for overspending. First, holiday shoppers are visiting retail stores, where temptations abound. The sights, sounds, and smells of a store, especially around the holidays, can create buying urges. Standing in front of an item allows your emotions to take over. It's the same as having good intentions to skip dessert during a restaurant dinner until the dessert tray comes and you succumb to the chocolate mousse.

Other emotional triggers are less obvious. For example, people are more likely to spend more when they're feeling especially good or bad, research shows. So, both holiday cheer and holiday stress contribute to spending.

Here are some ways to avoid holiday overspending:

- Shop online. That might sound like an unorthodox tip for saving money, but you can eliminate many of the triggers for overspending by not visiting a retail store at all. Nearly all the same merchandise is available over the Internet, where you can call up the item on the computer, order it, and have it shipped to you or the recipient. You have the added advantage of being able to get better prices by using shopping-comparison sites, or shop-bots, or simply surfing to several retailers in a matter of seconds. So, shopping online not only allows you to save money on what you buy but also reduces temptations, saving you money on items you might have purchased if you visited a store.

- Adhere to a budget. This is standard, though often ignored, advice. List the gift recipients and the amount to spend on each. Do not stray from that list. Research shows once you cheat a little with shopping, it's easier to start binge buying.

The planning part of creating a budget means you won't be frantically shopping at the last minute and overpaying just to get your shopping done.

- Keep holiday trips separate. Designate shopping trips for gift-shopping only. Don't mix a trip with household errands and personal shopping. Do the same for online shopping. Sit down at the computer and block off time for holiday shopping only. It will help you keep on task.

- Don't touch. Ever notice how some packaging allows you to touch the item through a cutout in the box? Research shows that if you handle a piece of merchandise and start envisioning it as your own, you're far more likely to buy it.

- Shop at the right time. If you will be shopping in person, avoid crowds by going during stores' early and late extended hours. Fewer crowds mean lower stress, which lowers the chance for impulse purchases. Another trick is to shop after 6 p.m. on the day before an advertised sale begins. Many retailers program their registers the evening before, meaning the sale price might already come up in the register even if sale signs aren't on the floor yet. You can also ask salespeople about when big-ticket items are likely to go on sale.

- Give cash or gift cards. This is another way to avoid the whole retail scene and its temptations. You'll have to decide whether cash or a gift card is appropriate. Be sure to read the rules for gift cards, including expiration dates.

Valentine's Day on the Cheap... Without Ending Up in the Doghouse

Many men perform few tasks worse than planning for Valentine's Day. And for men, trying to please a significant other without going broke is a struggle. That's not to say some women couldn't use a few excellent-but-frugal ideas too.

The keys to a successful Valentine's Day are creative and sincere reflections of love, which have nothing to do with money. But simply cheaping out on Valentine's Day can be dicey. Maybe that's why American consumers spent nearly $17 billion on Valentine's Day, or on average about $120 each, according to the National Retail Federation. The average man spends about $156, while the average woman spends about $85.

So, here are some ideas, some endearing, others purely practical, for the two primary parts of Valentine's Day—the date and the gift—that will put less strain on the budget without straining the relationship. They are geared more toward men because, as the spending statistics show, men need more help keeping the spending down.

The date:

- Move the celebration. Getting a baby-sitter or making a dinner reservation for February 14 or the prior weekend might be difficult. So suggest to your partner that you shift Valentine's Day to the following weekend. Besides making logistics easier, it allows you to get chocolates, cards, and flowers at deeply discounted post-Valentine's Day prices. However, it would be smart to plan some small gesture on the day itself, perhaps alluding to plans for the following weekend.

- Think dinner alternatives. Consider making dinner at home with your sweetheart's favorite dishes. Or make reservations at the fanciest restaurant in town but just for appetizers or dessert. You get the experience of elegant dining without the high price. Instead of dinner out, you could do a Valentine's breakfast, which is far cheaper. That works better if the breakfast kicks off a full day of planned Valentine's activities.

- Cheap dates are fun too. Instead of an expensive dinner or show, consider a date to a free art museum or concert or a trip to an aquarium or zoo. A park picnic in warm climates works. Or in colder regions, consider a date for snowshoeing or cross-country skiing, using rented or borrowed equipment. Bookstore browsing with coffee is nice. More unconventional is a fun date to visit auto dealerships and test-drive fancy cars, regardless of whether you're serious about buying—although you can debate the ethics of wasting a salesperson's time doing that.

- Pay attention to detail. Candles, incense, and music can set an ambience for a romantic date, even if it's at home. And they don't cost much.

The gift:

- Plan ahead. Scrambling for last-minute flowers and chocolates almost guarantees you'll spend more than you want to. And it ends up being a gesture of minimal sincerity.
- Play your cards right. More people buy greeting cards for Valentine's Day than any other holiday except Christmas, according to the Greeting Card Association. But they can be wildly expensive for what you get. Instead, a cheaper card from a dollar store, a homemade card made with paper and glue, or a card printed from the computer can substitute. However, that might come across as cheesy unless you come up with your own customized message. Ideas include a poem, a short essay on why you love her, or a top ten list about why she's the greatest.
- Cut down on candy. Who needs a giant box laden with empty carbohydrates and calories? Instead, go to a candy shop and buy one or two fancy pieces of candy. That satisfies the sweet tooth while cutting cost and calories.
- Consider flower options. Instead of buying a dozen red roses delivered to her for $80, stop at a local florist and buy her a single pink or yellow rose for $4. That may satisfy the flower requirement if it's part of a bigger planned celebration.
- Buy fake bling. Diamonds may be a girl's best friend, but costume jewelry with look-alike gemstones is nice too. Only a gem expert can tell the difference. A diamond tennis bracelet may cost nearly $10,000, but a look-alike with cubic zirconia stones could be had for $100 or less. Moissanite is more expensive than cubic zirconia, but it has more sparkle than a diamond and is a fraction of the price. Tell her you plan to one day replace it with real diamonds when you become wildly rich from spending your money smarter.

Ultimately, you'll have to decide the most appropriate way to show your love and get the best value for your money.

Tax Preparation: Frugal Ways to Pay Uncle Sam

It's bad enough that we have to pay federal taxes when the money sometimes goes to questionable expenditures. But it's even worse because the complexity of the tax code has us paying extra just to get the tax return filed.

Nine of ten U.S. taxpayers used either a professional preparer or a computer program to help prepare their taxes, according to the National Taxpayers Union. Table 7.2 shows how consumers have needed more and more help through the years. Out-of-pocket costs per individual taxpayer averaged $207 for tax preparation alone. That could be money well spent, given that you have no choice but to file a tax return. But some spending on tax preparation and filing is a huge waste. Following are a few tips—but not a comprehensive list—for spending less and getting better value for your money next tax season:

TABLE 7.2   Use of Paid Preparers and Computer Programs

Tax Year	Percent Who Paid for Human and Computer Preparers
1980	38%
1996	66%
2000	78%
2006	91%

Source: National Taxpayers Union

- Simple should mean cheap. Generally, the less complicated your tax situation, the less you should spend on tax preparation. If you want to hire a certified public accountant to fill out your 1040EZ form, you can. But it's a waste of money. In recent years, the tax preparation industry has started targeting young people, many of whom have simple tax situations. The pitch is that these on-the-go young people should attend to their important social engagements rather than spend a few minutes filling out a tax form. If you have no children, no mortgage, and work for someone else, you're a good candidate to do the simple return yourself and save on tax preparation costs.

- Check out Free File. If your income level qualifies for the IRS Free File program, try it. Free File offers online do-it-yourself tax preparation and electronic filing through companies that partnered with the IRS. For more information, go to www.irs.gov and click Free File. Be aware that doesn't mean it's free to file your state income taxes. In 2006, you qualified if your Adjusted Gross Income was $52,000 or less, which included some 95 million taxpayers, or 70 percent of all taxpayers.

- Books can be bargains. Tax advice books are relatively inexpensive help for tax preparation. Discovering a single additional deduction could more than pay for the cost of the book. Among those featured on many lists of best tax books for average people are the "Dummies" books co-written by Eric Tyson.

- Test-drive the software. Different tax-prep software appeals to different people. Go to leading online Web sites, such as www.turbotax.com, www.taxcut.com, and www.taxbrain.com, and start plugging your numbers into their online tax preparation programs. They are free to try. You pay only to e-file or print the return. Pay for the one that asks questions in a way that makes sense to you and helps you remember forgotten deductions. TurboTax and TaxCut come in desktop software versions too.

- Take advantage of free tax-prep services. Seniors and low-income taxpayers might be able to get free help with their tax returns through community organizations. Watch the local newspapers for such offers, keep an eye out in community newsletters, and if you're a senior check with the local senior center. Also check with the AARP program Tax-Aide for free in-person tax return help, www.aarp.org/money/taxaide, or 1-888-227-7669. Low- to moderate-income taxpayers may qualify for the Volunteer Income Tax Assistance Program (VITA). Call 1-800-829-1040 to find a local site. Those in the military qualify for free tax preparation from the Armed Forces Tax Council at offices within their installations.

- Hire a pro? Professional tax preparers, whether CPAs, enrolled agents, or other professional tax people, can more than pay for themselves. Their fee is worthwhile if they find ways for you to pay less tax and significantly reduce the hassle of tax preparation. Hiring a pro is a good idea if you had a significant change in the past year, such as buying or selling a house, starting a business, or retiring.

- Shop for a pro. There's nothing wrong with comparison shopping for a professional tax preparer. Fees vary widely. Ask about the total cost of preparation. Some chain stores suck you in with a low advertised price and then nickel-and-dime you for minor additional services.

- Don't pay to file electronically. The IRS loves e-filing because it cuts costs for the government, compared with paper tax returns. But it's not worth paying $20 to e-file when you could mail the tax return for the cost of a couple of postage stamps. Professional preparers should not charge you a separate fee for filing electronically. It's part of their cost of doing business.

- Forgo fast cash. Absolutely say "no" to refund anticipation loans. That's where a preparer gives you instant cash, based on your expected tax refund. But you're basically paying a fee to borrow your own money. These fees can amount to hundreds of percent interest. Besides, if you file electronically and have the money directly deposited to a bank account, you should have your refund inside of two weeks. You overpaid the government all year long. Why would it suddenly be urgent to have that money on the day you file your return?

- Spend your refund on paper first. You'll end up happier if you purposefully allocate refund money before it arrives, rather than just tossing it in the general-fund checking account where you will fritter it away on who-knows-what. For example, use half the money for debt reduction or savings, one quarter for a home or car repair, and the remaining quarter for fun money.

Wedding Gifts: An Invitation Is Not an Invoice

Attending weddings are mostly joyous occasions, but they can be stressful for guests on a tight budget who feel like they have to fork over a lavish wedding gift.

The average wedding gift costs $85, according to the Association of Bridal Consultants. Alone, that's not a big expense. But it becomes more significant if you already shelled out for an engagement gift, shower gift, and travel and lodging to get to a far-away wedding. Then, multiply that by several weddings in a year, and you're talking real money.

First, don't consider the wedding invitation an invoice for an expensive gift. Instead, base the gift's value on what you can afford and how well you know the couple. Presumably, you were invited to share in the couple's big day, not for how much you can add to the largess. The trick is to focus on giving a present the couple will appreciate without necessarily spending a bundle. At the same time, you want to adhere to gift-giving etiquette so you don't offend anyone.

Consider the following tips if you're on a tight budget:

- Avoid cash. Many couples appreciate gifts of money. It can defray the cost of the wedding or honeymoon, or contribute to a down payment on a house. But if you give cash, there's no way to hide the fact that you're trying to be frugal.

- Use the registry. Even if you choose something inexpensive off the wedding registry, you'll at least know the couple wants the gift. Don't buy a registry gift elsewhere for less money because that leads to duplicate gifts, and the couple will notice. Frankly, the idea with inexpensive gifts is to fly under the radar.

- Buy small. When buying off the registry, buy several small, inexpensive gifts. Frequently, guests don't choose to buy the small items, such as kitchen gadgets, even though the couple wants them.

- Top it off. Embellish a relatively inexpensive gift. If you're buying a $30 pasta pot, include a few boxes of gourmet pasta. If you're buying wine glasses, include a $20 bottle of wine. Both will look like $100 gift packages for half that price.

- Weight counts. Heavier gifts seem more expensive. So, consider inexpensive kitchen appliances such as blenders and toaster ovens.

- Buddy up. Coordinate with other guests to pool money and buy an expensive item on the registry, something the couple doesn't really expect to get. You look like a hero because you were partly responsible for a dream gift, but you could actually spend less than if you bought a cheaper separate item.

- Get personal. If you know the couple well, assemble an inexpensive gift you know will be meaningful or especially useful. Just be certain it doesn't duplicate something on the registry. Buy gifts associated with their hobbies, whether camping, gardening, or listening to country music. Or sign them up for a local wine-tasting class, if that's what they enjoy.

- Save on shipping. When buying a gift from an online registry, have it shipped directly to the couple, rather than to yourself. If you take delivery, you'll just have to repackage it and forward it to the bride and groom.

Kid Birthday Parties: Rein in the Ridiculous

Children's birthdays nowadays just aren't what they used to be. Instead of a simple party with family, friends, and a cake, a party can include pony rides, a backyard petting zoo, or professional magician. Some parties are held at bowling alleys, laser tag facilities, and the local arcade-and-pizza joint.

That change means parties are more expensive. Americans spend some $10 billion a year on birthdays, according to greeting card company Hallmark. And children's birthday parties are a big part of that.

More birthday expense arises when your child attends a friend's party and has to come bearing a gift. Here are tips for reining in the cost of your child's party and the cost of gifts your child buys for friends:

- Money can't buy you love. Spending a lot of money on your child's party has nothing to do with making it more enjoyable or memorable. Instead, it has to be a meaningful event, whether going to a baseball game, a play, or the zoo with the family and perhaps one friend. A picnic in the park is a good idea for young children because they usually prefer to run around and play their own games instead of participating in structured activities.

- Buddy up. A rule of thumb is to invite one friend for every year of the child's age. A five-year-old would have five friends. But sometimes parents will invite a child's entire school class to a party, which puts pressure on other parents to do the same. One idea is to collaborate with other parents whose children have birthdays in the same month. Host a single big party and invite the whole class. The cost and hassle of planning the party can be spread among several parents.

- Set spending limits. It may seem overkill to set a budget for a party or for year-round children's gifts, but a spending plan can help parents plan their finances and avoid impulse buys. Older children might appreciate a party budget if you let them choose how the money is spent. Give them power to allocate the money among party favors, decorations, refreshments, entertainment, and other parts of the event. That way, planning the party becomes part of the birthday memory.

  A budget is also important for buying gifts for another child's birthday party. Set a budget of between $10 and $20, for example, and let your child choose a gift in that price range. That has the added benefit of being a lesson about living on a budget.

- Skip the card. Most kids won't appreciate a $5 birthday greeting card and fancy wrapping paper. So forgo the card or give a handwritten note instead. And wrap a gift in the Sunday comic section of the newspaper. Similarly, most four-year-old boys won't care whether the plastic cups match the paper plates, so don't bother spending extra to coordinate disposable partyware.

- Make the usual unusual. For example, keep refreshments simple and inexpensive, but give them fancy names, suggests Hallmark on its Web site. A baseball theme lends itself to "home-run hot dogs" and "pop-fly popcorn," and a magic theme calls for "celestial cupcakes with stardust sparkles" and "magic pink lemonade."

- Think nonmaterial gifts. Take a day off from work and bring your child to a museum or give him a new privilege, such as a later bedtime or curfew. Or talk with your child about taking a year off from birthday gifts. Instead, encourage friends, relatives, and partygoers to donate money or a toy that will go to a charity. The child can then go in person to present the donation and enjoy the thrill of giving.

Amusement Parks: Costs Shouldn't Take You for a Ride

Amusement parks can be a fun family getaway, but too many families needlessly overspend for their day of roller coasters and water slides.

An admission ticket to a regional amusement park often costs about $50. Add parking, refreshments, and a host of other expenses, and a family of four could easily spend $300 on a one-day outing.

Most times you can save a lot of money with just a little planning. Here are some tips for spending less on amusement parks. Some also apply to such attractions as the zoo, museum, and aquarium.

- Never pay retail. Listed admission prices are for suckers or people who just don't care about wasting money. They're like a new car's sticker price that nobody actually expects you to pay. In fact, some parks are raising rates only to boast that they're offering bigger discounts, knowing some consumers care more about the discount than the final price.

- Use a coupon. In most cases, if you can't find a coupon for a discounted admission price, you're not trying hard enough.

Many parks will give you a discount just for going to their Web sites. Other places to look are on soft drink cans, in the newspaper, AAA, your warehouse club, and at your employer's human resources office.

- Planning 101. Check out all the latest promotions on the park's Web site and then phone the park. Ask the guest relations person about discounts and promotions the park is offering. While on the phone, inquire about how crowded the park is likely to be on the day you want to go and whether any special events, such as parades, music concerts, corporate picnics, or fireworks are happening that day. You may decide to alter your plans to attend on a Sunday instead of Saturday, for example, to avoid crowds.

- Recruit friends. Most parks offer group rates, some for as few as ten people. If you plan a trip to a park with a few neighbors, you could not only get the group rate but also save on parking and gasoline if you carpool with a large vehicle or two.

- Time it right. Arrive first thing in the morning when the gates open to avoid crowds. Alternatively, try after 5 p.m. when you could qualify for a cheap late-day pass and crowds will be subsiding. The best days of the week to go are Tuesdays through Thursdays to avoid weekend crowds. And the best time of the year is September, followed by early April. Even Labor Day weekend might be okay because most families are in back-to-school mode and are mentally finished with their summer fun.

- Go against the grain. Avoiding crowds will give you better value for your amusement park buck. Upon entering the park, get a map and develop a game plan. If one ride in particular intrigues you, go there first thing in the morning and get your fill. Other strategies are to head for the back of the park and work your way forward, avoiding the crowds, or after entering the front gate, make a left and continue clockwise around the park, which is the opposite of what most people do. Eat before 11 a.m. or after 1 p.m. if you're buying food at the park. You'll avoid lines at food vendors and be on the rides while many others are eating lunch.

- Bring food. Usually, you can't bring refreshments into a park, but you can exit the main gate and come back in. So, avoid overpriced and poor-quality food by keeping a cooler of food and drinks in the car. Some amusement parks even offer picnic grounds near the parking lot. So, try to land a parking spot near the picnic area. Inside the park, you may be able to bring a bottle to refill at water fountains.

- Go easy in the gift shop. Give kids a limit for gift shop purchases and save shopping for the end of the day. That way, you avoid lugging the items around all day and possibly the cost of renting a locker. Hit the front-gate gift store on the way out. It will have a variety of the best items and provides one-stop shopping. If you're on a tight household budget, you want to skip the gift shop altogether.

Vacation Accommodations: Hotel Versus Home Rental

Vacation planning often involves choosing among hotels and motels near your destination. But you have other choices for accommodations.

Whether headed to the beach, the mountains, a lake, or a theme park, more families are renting full vacation houses, cabins, and villas. Surprisingly, rental homes—besides being much more spacious—can be less expensive than renting a hotel room.

In fact, renting a house instead of a hotel room is often a better choice. Renting a whole house or condominium is a familiar concept for those who regularly vacation in some parts of the country, such as East Coast beach locations. But in other regions, the idea of renting a vacation home is just catching on.

A vacation home rental might be the smartest way to spend your vacation dollars. Here's what to consider:

- Size of your party. Generally, if you're traveling with three or more people and have to get at least two hotel rooms, a home rental will be cheaper. You'll get a lot more space, often with

multiple bedrooms and bathrooms, and bigger living and dining areas. In some expensive markets, rentals are cheaper than
a single hotel room of comparable luxury. Envision a 250-
square-foot hotel room with two double beds and a rollaway for
the same price as an 1,800-square-foot, three-bedroom house.
With more space, you'll be comfortable just relaxing, rather
than feel like you have to be away from the small hotel room
and on the go. And people accustomed to their 3,000 square-
foot houses—or larger—might feel cramped in a hotel room all
week.

- Eating in. Having a kitchen in a vacation rental means you'll
  have to eat out less often. Dining out for every meal is not only
  expensive and time consuming but also can be a stressful hassle
  if you have a large group or young children. Sometimes, a quick
  breakfast of coffee and cold cereal or a bagel before hitting the
  beach might be more enjoyable than waiting for a table at a
  restaurant every morning.

- Amenities. With a vacation rental, you won't have daily house-
  keeping, concierge service, room service dining, and a fitness
  center, but you might have use of a grill on a patio, beach chairs
  and beach toys, bicycles, and kitchen appliances and utensils.
  You might have a free washer and dryer, which allows you to
  pack fewer clothes. Vacation rentals are more likely to have
  video players, board games, and books to keep kids occupied
  on rainy days. And, like many hotel rooms, rentals might have
  Internet access included.

- Minor chores. With vacation rentals, you might have to put
  sheets on the beds when you arrive and take out the garbage
  during the week, among other small tasks. Of course, that's
  unnecessary with hotels.

- Privacy. A vacation rental's walled-off rooms with doors means
  adults can steal some "alone time," away from children or other
  people in your vacation party. And separate rooms facilitate
  young children's naps and early bedtimes.

- Pets. Many vacation rentals allow pets, which can save you
  money on kennel costs. In general, rentals that allow pets will
  be nicer than hotels that do.

- Ease of reservations. Hotels win on this count because you can call toll-free numbers anytime or even book on the Internet. However, booking vacation rentals has become easier with such Web sites as HomeAway.com and its affiliates VRBO.com, CyberRentals.com, and GreatRentals.com. Others are VacationHomes.com and vacationhomerentals.com, but you can find more with an Internet search engine. Searching through home rentals takes more time than choosing a hotel, but it's potentially more fun too, almost like house shopping.

- Flexibility. Pay-by-the-night hotels offer the most time flexibility, and you can cancel on short notice. But you don't always have to commit to a weeklong stay at a vacation rental. Many homeowners will let you rent by the weekend or even on a nightly basis, particularly during the off-season. Most still expect you to pay by personal check, but others accept credit cards or online payment system PayPal.

- Risk. Dealing with individual homeowners carries more risk than doing business with established hotel chains. So at first, maintain a skeptical attitude by asking a lot of questions and insisting on a written contract. Ask if the property is professionally cleaned between rental periods. Use Web sites that charge homeowners for a listing, rather than free listing services. Pay sites might do at least cursory checking to make sure the vacation property actually exists and may ban listings that garner complaints. And if the property is listed through a property management agency, it's less likely to be a scam.

In sum, if you're after the best value for the money in terms of space and home-away-from-home living, rentals are the way to go. They're especially good for families and large groups. But if you're into simplicity and pampering—and money is less of an issue—then hotels still represent the best choice.

8

Life Happens:
Big-Ticket Infrequent Spending

While it's important to pay attention to the little daily spending that adds up, you can't ignore the big monster expenses that happen less often. We all know what they are: cars, homes, weddings, medical bills, and the like.

These large infrequent expenditures are prime areas for saving a bundle of money at one time. But they're also areas that much is written about, and information is readily available. So, I'll try to give you overall concepts about this type of spending.

For some topics, I'll put first things first. For example, the first question in buying a car is not, "What car do I want?" Instead, it is, "How much can I spend?" followed by "What car do I want for the money I can afford to spend?" It seems elementary, but it's crucial to think about cars and other large expenditures in that way, in that order. In fact, cars are the source of so many spending problems that I've included two sections on the subject.

In other sections, such as moving costs and getting a divorce, I'll point out some specific money-saving tactics.

The following tips aren't the be-all and end-all about these subjects. After all, entire books are written about buying cars, buying homes, planning weddings, and paying college tuition. But the advice here will give you plenty of ideas for spending smarter when life happens.

How Much Car Can I Afford?—Less Than You Think

For many consumers, the logic goes like this:

"I need a vehicle for transportation."

"New vehicles cost about $30,000."

"I must spend about $30,000 for a vehicle."

The problem is the third notion, the conclusion. It's lazy thinking that stems from "wants"—car lust—rather than an analysis of "needs"—transportation.

"The worst auto accidents you'll ever see occur on the showroom floor," says get-out-of-debt specialist Dave Ramsey, author of *The Total Money Makeover*.

Those accidents happen as consumers sign up for years of crippling debt to buy vehicles they can't afford. Americans have quickly gotten used to new car prices starting north of $30,000. The fixation seems to be on the car payment. Consumers figure, "I'll always have a car payment. Everybody has one." That's why they don't even care what the car costs or how many years they'll be paying it off. They only care about the monthly payment.

If that sounds like your attitude, you might have fallen for the car payment debt trap, the never-ending cycle of financing automobiles. It robs many Americans of their potential wealth because they're funneling a huge portion of their incomes into an asset that's plummeting in value.

Can you afford the car you have right now? Think carefully. That's a different question than "Can you make your payments so the car doesn't get repossessed?" It means, "Can you afford your car so it fits comfortably in your financial life and isn't driving your financial priorities?"

The key is to first figure out what you can afford before you go to the car lot, instead of trying to fit your household budget around the pricey vehicle you just bought.

Here are six signs that your automobile might be too expensive for you:

- You bought a new car. Depreciation is the 30 percent in value your new car loses during the first year of ownership. On a $30,000 vehicle, that's a $9,000 loss. If $9,000 is pocket change for you, then you can afford a new car. If $9,000 is a lot of money in your world, you'll need a less expensive car. It's not a more difficult analysis than that. For most people, that will mean buying a used car. A more modestly priced example of a Toyota Camry is in Table 8.1.

TABLE 8.1   Costs of a Base-Model Toyota Camry

	Price	**Savings Compared with New MSRP**
2008 Camry	$20,280	$—
2005 Camry	$13,285	$ 6,995
2002 Camry	$9,395	$10,885

Source: Kelley Blue Book

- You financed the car. Here's a harsh statement: If you cannot pay for a car in cash, you cannot afford the car. "But," you counter, "Where am I going to get money to pay cash for a car?" That's the wrong question. The question is, "Where do I find a car to buy with the cash I have?" One answer is the cash-only, trade-up plan. It goes something like this: Keep your current car for at least three years after paying it off. After paying it off, continue making monthly car payments to yourself, perhaps in a separate bank account. When you need a new car, buy one for the price of your savings plus the sale value of your old car. Repeat this process every few years, and you'll regularly trade up to a more expensive vehicle while paying cash.

- Your car payment is too high. Although paying cash is ideal, most people will refuse to heed that advice. So when is a car payment too high? Many experts suggest all your car payments should add up to less than 15 percent of monthly take-home pay. Let's assume that's a good rule of thumb. That means a family with the median U.S. annual household income of $46,242 might take home about 75 percent of that, or about $34,700. That family can afford total car payments of $434, which would get you one $14,000 car, assuming no down payment or trade-in and a three-year loan. *By that math, the typical household in America can't afford half the price of today's new cars.*

  The other rule of thumb, mentioned in Chapter 4, "The Big Picture," is even stricter. It suggests car payments should not exceed 7 percent of *gross* income—and that's if you have no other debt. That means the median U.S. household could afford total car payments of about $270.

- You financed for more than three years. Assuming you won't pay cash for the vehicle, determine whether the payment for a three-year car loan is too much for your household budget to handle comfortably. If so, the car might be too expensive for you. If you must finance a car for longer than four years, it's definitely too expensive. Instead of financing for a longer period to reduce the payment, get a smaller payment by purchasing a less expensive car.

- You leased the car to get a lower payment. This is a tell-tale sign you bought too much car. Few auto leases are worthwhile for most people and almost never make good financial sense.

- Your vehicles total half your income. The total current value of all your cars—plus boats, motorcycles, and similar vehicles—should be less than half your gross annual household income, according to a Dave Ramsey rule of thumb. That's regardless of whether you own the vehicle outright or are still making finance payments. So, if your household income is the U.S. median of $46,242, the total value of all your vehicles should not be more than about $23,000. You can find the current value of vehicles at such Web sites as Kelley Blue Book, www.kbb.com. The idea is you need to limit the amount of money you have tied up in assets that are going down in value.

So, what do you do if your car is too expensive for you? If you're near the end of the loan term, you might suck it up and keep paying the loan, vowing never again to buy a car you can't afford.

If your vehicles are sinking your finances, consider selling one or more vehicles. Sell privately instead of trading in to get the most money you can. Then buy a far less expensive used car. If you're "upside down" on the vehicle, meaning you owe more than the car is worth, get a personal loan for the difference so you can sell it and buy a cheaper one. Your best bet might be a loan from a credit union. It's better to owe a few thousand dollars to the credit union than tens of thousands to the auto financing company.

If you don't look closely at your automobile expenses, you'll be literally driving away your wealth.

Why Buy Used? You're Not Buying Someone Else's Problem

Few events in life offer a better chance to waste money than buying a car or truck. And the ultimate in overspending is purchasing a brand-new vehicle.

Don't be offended if you're one of the millions of Americans who buy only new cars. Years ago, there were good reasons to stay away from used cars.

But times have changed, and so should your attitude toward used cars if you want to spend your money more wisely.

It's not news that the value of new cars, trucks, vans, and SUVs falls off a cliff the minute you drive it from the dealer's lot. That moment can cost you 20 percent of the car's value, or $5,000 on a $25,000 car. So, that "new" car is worth just $20,000 on the used-car market in minute No. 2 of ownership. Then through the first year of the car's life, its value drops by another 10 percent, according to Edmunds.com.

That's paying a huge premium for new-car smell.

Smart spending dictates you let someone else absorb the profoundly poor investment of buying new, while you swoop in later for the value. It can be especially prudent if you are determined to buy a luxury car you can't really afford to buy new. Buying used is the ideal solution.

In fact, for all car buyers, purchasing a used vehicle makes more sense today than ever before. That's because many of the arguments against buying a pre-owned car just don't hold up anymore. Here's why:

- Quality. The most common objection to buying used is "I don't want to buy someone else's problem." Previously, buying a three- or four-year-old vehicle meant you would own it just in time for a series of mechanical problems to develop, which required expensive repairs. But the quality of cars today is the best ever. Years ago, a car's life petered out at 100,000 miles. Today, reliable cars can last almost twice that long. Many Honda Accords, an example of ultra-reliable sedans, are likely to go 150,000 miles with just normal maintenance.

- Warranties. Some bumper-to-bumper warranties cover four years or 50,000 miles, and powertrain warranties can last ten years or 100,000 miles. That's much more extensive coverage than a generation ago. Many warranties are transferable to secondary owners, although it's important to check the details.

- Used-car glut. There are more and better used cars for sale because they're coming off leases. And because of low financing rates and high rebates in recent years, some car buyers have traded in late-model cars for even newer ones. That leaves many gently used, low-mileage cars for the used-car market, leading to greater choice and relatively lower prices.

- Information. You can know exactly what you should pay for a used car by using free online Web sites, including Edmunds.com and Kelley Blue Book, www.kbb.com. *Consumer Reports* offers a report for $10. And unlike years ago, today you can get a report about the vehicle's history. You just supply the vehicle identification number (VIN). The report, many available instantly online, will tell you whether the car was totaled, detail its mileage and ownership history, and tell you whether it was involved in a fire or flood. One good source is a $20 report from Carfax, www.carfax.com.

- New marketplaces. For-sale signs on the windshield, newspaper classifieds, and even new-car dealerships are still good places to search for used cars, but today there are more options. Online auctions, especially at eBay.com, can be a good source of used cars at good prices. It can even pay to buy cars in far-away places in the United States and either pay to ship it or buy a one-way plane ticket to pick up the car and drive it back. Online classified ads are available at a number of Web sites. Large car-buying sites include, www.autobytel.com, www.autotrader.com, www.carsdirect.com, and www.autos.msn.com.

- Certified pre-owned. If you're nervous and want to dip a toe into the used-car pool, consider a used car certified by the manufacturer. With a factory-certified used car, you'll pay more, maybe about $2,000 more, but you should get an extended warranty, and you can rest easier knowing you're getting the cream of the used-car crop. More importantly, it will make you feel more comfortable buying used cars in the future. Just be very clear about what "certified" means and get details. Manufacturer warranties are far superior to car-lot warranties.

Make no mistake, buying a used car is a little—or a lot—more work. It could include more research and requires the legwork of getting the car evaluated by a mechanic. And a private-party transaction will require you to handle the paperwork of transferring the car's ownership. In most cases, however, your effort will be handsomely rewarded with hundreds, or even thousands, of dollars in savings.

If you're convinced that buying your next car used is the best idea, then choose at least three models to pursue to maintain flexibility. Also, consider quality cars that don't hold their value well because they've already suffered their greatest depreciation. If you like late models, own a car during the sweet spot of its lifecycle, buying at year No. 2 and selling at year No. 5. Of course, buying used and holding it for a decade is a great idea too.

Buying used cars instead of new ones can be the smartest spending decision you make in your lifetime.

How Much House Can I Afford? Don't Be "House Poor"

Buying a house is a fabulous idea and remains part of many people's definition of living the "American Dream."

In the past, it often ended up being the single best spending decision many Americans ever made.

Perhaps the most startling statistic comes from looking at people's ultimate measure of wealth, called net worth. It's simply all you own, minus all you owe. American homeowners have a median net worth of $184,400, while renters are worth $4,000, according to the most recent 2004 figures from the Federal Reserve.

But homeownership alone is not a panacea, especially in an era of easy lending and complicated home loans. Those recent changes have led many consumers to buy houses they simply cannot afford, which leads to the gut-wrenching process of foreclosure.

Here are some considerations when buying a home:

- Know the mortgage you can afford. The Federal Housing Administration, the government agency that helps people buy homes by guaranteeing loans, has a formula for home affordability. Mortgage principal and interest, plus real estate taxes, plus homeowner's insurance should not exceed 29 percent of your gross income. That means a family with $75,000 in income could afford a house payment of about $1,800.

  And your total debt, including the mortgage, car loans, credit cards, and the like, should not exceed 41 percent, according to FHA. That also means if you have no debt, you could technically afford a mortgage and associated costs of up to 41 percent of gross income.

However, that's a liberal, and even risky, formula. You would be safer keeping those total expenses, plus additional maintenance costs, to about a third of your *take-home* pay, which delivers a very different—and lower—affordability figure.

More conservative yet is that the house payment should not exceed a quarter of your take-home pay on a 15-year fixed-rate mortgage.

Mortgage affordability calculators abound on the Internet. Run your numbers through a dozen of them to get a feel for what price range you should be looking at. Start with calculators at Bankrate.com and Dinkytown.com and use your favorite search engine to find others.

- Don't think "dream home." You may one day live in your dream home, with the luxurious back porch, the granite countertops, or the whirlpool bath, but it's unlikely to be your first home or even your third. The priority is to get into something you can afford, and then work on trading up or improving the house you have. While home shopping, avoid the temptation to visit homes for sale outside your price range.

- You don't need a huge down payment. Getting together enough cash for a 20 percent down payment is a good idea, but unnecessary anymore. Putting down less cash should be okay in a decent housing market, as long as you're conservative on the size of your mortgage. Saving at least $5,000 to $10,000 to put down on a small house will be a signal to yourself that you're serious about being a homeowner. If you're wondering where to get money for the down payment, you need only to read other parts of this book to spend your money smarter.

- Do your research. Buying a home is likely the single biggest purchase you'll make, so it's worth doing research. Know the housing market, read about and compare mortgage financing options, and always do the math on whatever home-buying topic comes up. If you're not willing to do the learning and work, you're not ready to be a responsible homeowner.

If you can't yet afford to buy a home, don't dismay. You're not the sinner many people will make you out to be. You will not be forced to wear a scarlet letter "R" for "renter." If you're concerned about the difference in cost between buying and renting, plug in numbers to an online calculator by mortgage-backer Ginnie Mae at www.ginniemae.gov.

Possible reasons to continue renting are that you don't want the hassle and added expense of maintaining a home, or you want the flexibility to move your residence quickly. Or your might be convinced your area is experiencing a real estate bubble that soon will see depreciating prices, and rents are relatively inexpensive.

Or the best reason is that you're continuing to rent until you shape up your finances enough so that you're in a position to buy a home and start achieving your own "American Dream."

Moving Costs: Getting Your Stuff from Here to There

Moving your belongings into a new apartment or house can be physically, emotionally, and financially draining. Today, do-it-yourselfers have a plethora of choices for trading off cost with hassle.

Full-service interstate moves can be outrageously expensive, while a total self-move can be stressful and back wrenching. So it pays to know what help is available and how to cut out unnecessary expense, whether for a local move costing several hundred dollars or a coast-to-coast full-service move costing thousands.

Beware that the moving business, which handles 40 million household moves each year, has more than its share of scam artists. Here are some tips on saving money and avoiding scams:

- Get your employer to pay. If you're moving for a job, try to get all you can in reimbursement of moving expenses. A full relocation package is ideal, but anything you can negotiate is just free money. Also, keep your receipts. Some expenses may be tax deductible. To see the tax rules for moving expenses, go online to www.irs.gov and search for IRS Publication 521, called "Moving Expenses."

- Be flexible on timing. May through September and the beginning and the end of each month are busy times for moving companies and truck rentals, which means they may be more expensive than during off times. A midmonth winter move might yield the best deal, if you have that flexibility. It can be a doubly good value because you're also likely to get a better moving crew during off-peak times.

- Chuck it. Because full-service moving companies charge by the pound, the less stuff you take the cheaper it will be. And if you move yourself, it could mean renting a smaller truck and saving money, or at least lugging less stuff out of your old digs and into your new place. Use a critical eye as you go through possessions and be ruthless about throwing stuff out, donating it, or selling it at a yard sale. That's especially important for heavy items, such as pool tables, sectional furniture, and exercise equipment.

- Get freebies. You might want special packing boxes for valuables, but free boxes from the grocery store or elsewhere work fine for transporting your more durable possessions, such as books and CDs. And it will save money on moving supplies.

- Supply your own packing materials. Wardrobe boxes, packing tape, bubble wrap, and similar products might be cheaper to buy at a self-moving company such as U-Haul International, Inc., or a shipping-supply company rather than buying directly from the moving company you're using.

- Pack stuff yourself. You can save hundreds of dollars by packing most of your belongings yourself. An exception would be fragile and valuable items, which you might want packed by a professional. There are two reasons. First, the items are less likely to be broken or damaged if packed by a pro in packing materials designed for fragile items. And second, many movers won't insure boxes you packed yourself.

- "You load, we haul." This is a hybrid option, where you pack belongings yourself, and the trucking company drops off a trailer at your house for a couple of days so you can load it.

Then a professional driver will pick it up and drive it to your new home, where he drops it, and you unload it yourself. This might be an especially good idea for those who want to move themselves but are nervous about driving a large truck.

- Beware of low-ball estimates. Get at least three price quotes for full-service moves, with an eye toward companies recommended by friends and relatives. Be skeptical of price quotes that far undercut competitors. It may be a sign the mover will come up with extra charges once he has your possessions locked in his truck. He will essentially hold the stuff hostage until you pay a ransom. You can increase your chances of finding a reputable company if you make sure it's a member of the American Moving and Storage Association, www.moving.org, or 703-683-7410.

- Spot a scammer. If a moving company wants to charge by the cubic foot rather than weight, it's a dead giveaway that the company may not be reputable. Be careful of a mover that doesn't agree to an on-site inspection of your household goods and gives an estimate only over the phone or Internet. And be suspicious of moving companies that demand cash only or a large deposit before the move. For helpful information on interstate moves, see Web sites for the Federal Motor Carrier Safety Administration, www.protectyourmove.gov, or the American Moving and Storage Association.

Wedding Spending: Like Marriage, It's About Compromise

It's pleasant to think about a fairy-tale wedding where nobody mentions the word budget, where money is no object. But then, it's more pleasant to think about a fairy-tale marriage where never a harsh word is spoken and you live out your love-struck days in eternal bliss.

That ain't happening either.

Weddings can be extremely expensive. The average cost of a traditional American wedding is pushing $30,000, with costs in pricey regions such as New York totaling much more.

But a secret of the wedding industry is that a lot of those dollars are spent on items and services that won't make much difference to the couple or the guests. The key is to scrutinize every aspect of the wedding, starting with the invitations and paying special attention to the most expensive part, the reception. Then determine whether the couple will get significant value from each expense. If not, cut it out or substitute something cheaper.

It's about choosing priorities, about spending your money on what's important to you. Insisting on having the best of everything is an immature attitude and just not practical. You will always have to cheap out on something. The good news is you get to decide.

Here is advice on spending money smarter when planning a wedding, with help from folks at TheKnot.com and Alan and Denise Fields, authors of several books on weddings.

- Revere the B word. Not bride—budget. Come up with a total dollar figure and use industry averages as a guide to break down how much you should spend in each area. TheKnot.com has a budget calculator on its Web site. For example, with a $25,000 wedding and 150 guests, it suggests spending $1,500 on the wedding dress, $2,000 on alcohol, and $1,500 on the reception band or disc jockey. Of course, you customize those areas to whatever is most important to you. Having a budget also makes dealing with vendors easier. For example, give the florist a dollar figure for all the flowers and provide the colors you like. Let him do the work of sorting through choices and presenting you with options.
- Be creative. If you're shopping at traditional wedding outlets, you're almost sure to overpay, especially if the retailer's name has the word "wedding" in it. To be creative, you might have to lose attitudes about the proper place to buy things. For

example, Costco, the big warehouse club, is a great place to get diamond engagement rings for less. Buying a wedding dress from an online retailer or mail order can save money, as can renting a limousine from a funeral home.

- Make sure the time is right. The bride may always have dreamed of a June wedding, but if she can be flexible enough to hold it during a less popular time of the year, the savings can be substantial. You can have a more lavish wedding for the same price if you'll hold it during a less expensive time of year. Similarly, avoiding the usual Saturday evening wedding is sure to reap savings. An earlier wedding and a lunch or brunch reception can save a bundle. And for Christian church weddings, consider Christmastime nuptials. The church is already decorated with holiday flowers, which cuts out an entire category of expense.

- Trim multiplied expenses. Spending cuts that involve guests can be big savers because even a small savings turns big when multiplied by the number of guests. For a wedding with 200 guests, a small $5-per-guest savings reaps $1,000. And if you can cut down the guest list, it means big savings at the reception—on food, alcohol, table centerpieces, and other costs. You can cut the food cost-per-guest by bringing in an outside caterer if the reception venue will allow it.

- Save on blooms. Take an especially hard look at your flowers category. Most people don't notice flowers and can't tell whether a red bloom is a rose or a carnation from 10 or 20 yards away. So, choose a color, not a specific flower. Overall, try to cut in half the price of the florist's first suggestion by substituting less expensive flowers. And you can easily eliminate or reduce the size of the huge bridal bouquet, which mostly gets in the way of seeing the bride. Use potted plants instead of floral arrangements at the reception, where it's usually dark anyway. A rented plant might cost $150 when a large floral arrangement could cost up to $750.

- Dress success. Order the designer dress of your dreams but ask for it in a less expensive fabric. Nobody will know the difference, and you could save $500. Cut down on the embroidery and save another $1,000 on high-end dresses. If you're at all handy, make the bridal veil for $10, rather than spending $500.

Also, check out sample sales for dresses in December and January, when wedding salons sell floor display models to make room for new shipments. A $5,000 new dress might cost $1,500 as a "sample."

- Piece-of-cake savings. Instead of a large wedding cake, get a small one for photos. After the obligatory wedding-cake photos, wheel the cake out of view and have the wait staff serve individual helpings from an undecorated sheet cake stashed in the kitchen. A sheet cake can cost 75 percent less because it's not decorated, and guests won't know the difference. Marie Antoinette had it right—let them eat cake. Why serve a dessert course at the reception dinner when there's cake?

- Booze budget. Don't stock brand-name liquor in the open bar. Few people will notice the difference after the first drink anyway. Limit what the open bar includes. If you cut down to beer and wine only, add at least one special cocktail and give it a clever name that means something to the wedding couple.

- Easy cuts and trade-offs. Forgo hand-done calligraphy for the outside of wedding invitations and all the layers of enclosures. Cut the limousine service. Or consider using a rented or borrowed luxury car. There's no need for floral arrangements in the bathrooms of the reception facility, despite your florist's urgings. Go with simple reception-party hors d'oeuvres and splurge on the entrees instead. Say no to the fancy cases and albums for the wedding video and photos. They can cost hundreds of dollars. You can buy nice ones much cheaper. And if you're going with live music, don't hire a separate band for cocktail hour. Instead, hire a few members of the reception band to come early.

- Buyer beware. Surely, the majority of wedding vendors earn their money, but be on guard for rip-offs. For example, some hotels and country clubs have ridiculous charges, such as "cake-cutting fees," which cost 50 cents to $2 per guest simply for slicing the wedding cake. Some florists change the price of wedding flowers based on what type of car drives up. Show up in a BMW, and you might pay top dollar. Gown preservation services that promise to clean and preserve the wedding dress are mostly a rip-off. Most dress shops simply throw the gown into a regular washing machine in the back of the store.

And preserving the dress for a daughter is a nice idea, but it rarely happens. Just 2 percent of brides wear a family heirloom dress, surveys show.

* Where not to skimp. After the music has faded away, the food is eaten, and the flowers are wilted and gone, all you have left is your memories, captured on film and video. Don't skimp on photography. To cut photography costs, use a professional photographer for the ceremony, but not for the reception. Instead, place disposable cameras on the tables and have guests take pictures.

College Tuition: The Two-Year, Two-Year Plan

College costs continue to rise far ahead of inflation, often saddling parents with huge tuition bills or the student with suffocating student loans.

But high school students and their parents should consider one particularly good alternative: a community college as an economical starting point for a four-year degree.

The idea is that students who intend to pursue a four-year bachelor's degree can complete their introductory coursework at a two-year school. Students can then transfer to a four-year school as a junior and graduate with a bachelor's degree.

Using total-expense statistics for the 2006-07 school year from the College Board and multiplied by four years, here is a breakdown of the choices in round numbers: private college, $133,000; two-year school, then private college, $79,000; public college, $65,000; two-year school, then finishing at a four-year public college, $45,000. Single-year price differences are highlighted in Table 8.2.

TABLE 8.2 Annual College Prices Vary Dramatically

School	Tuition and fees	Books and supplies	Room and board	Trans-portation	Other expenses	Total expenses
Two-year public college	$2,272	$850		$1,197	$1,676	$5,995
Four-year public college	$5,836	$942	$6,960	$880	$1,739	$16,357
Four-year private college	$22,218	$935	$8,149	$722	$1,277	$33,301

Source: The College Board 2006-2007
Note: Two-year college figures assume commuting to campus. Four-year college figures assume residing on campus. Public college assumes state residency.

That two-year/two-year plan nets out to about a $55,000 savings for private school and $21,000 savings for public school. Savings figures exclude room and board costs for living at home for two years. In other words, it assumes mom and dad would allow the student to live and eat at home free. Here are financial reasons to consider attending a community college for the first two years of a four-year program:

- You pay for it regardless. On average, 70 percent of community college expenses are covered by taxes, according to the American Association of Community Colleges.
- Two years at half price. Tuition and fees at public community colleges average less than half of those at public four-year colleges and about one-tenth of those at private four-year colleges.
- Results are good. Studies show that students who spend their first two years at a community college and then go on to graduate from a four-year college are as well prepared academically as those who go directly to a four-year college, according to the College Board. Research also shows students who take the community college route earn just as much money after they graduate.

- Favorable teaching conditions. Community college students learn in relatively small classes from instructors whose primary responsibility is teaching, not research. Many teachers have extensive "real-world" experience in their subject areas. And the average student-teacher contact time is higher at community colleges.

- The stigma has faded. Negative stereotypes about community colleges from previous generations have changed. And consider that in using the two-year/two-year plan, a bachelor's degree is issued by the four-year college. The diploma doesn't mention being a "transfer student."

- Live cheaply at home. The community college route not only has lower tuition and fees, but it avoids the expensive cost of housing and food at a four-year school. For community college, the cost of room and board would be basically groceries and transportation. That's likely to be far less than the $7,000 per year for room and board at a state school or $8,100 annually for a private university.

- Ability to work. Community college course schedules are flexible, which might help students work their way through school easier than at a four-year school.

- Fickle protection. Many 18-year-olds don't know exactly what career path they want to pursue or whether college is right for them at all. Exploring their career choices is a lot cheaper at community college rates.

- Lower student loan bills. Many graduates of four-year schools are saddled with enormous student loans, amounting to tens of thousands of dollars. That debt will burden them for years after graduation, affecting what houses and cars they can afford, for example. Lower college costs allow students to dig out of that hole quicker.

However, there at least a few possible reasons to pay more money for four years at a state or private college. It's up to you to put a price tag on how much they're worth:

- You don't have to worry about whether a student's academic credits earned in the first two years will apply toward a four-year degree. Rules for transferring credits are spelled out in "articulation agreements" between colleges.

- Many community college students will need a vehicle to get to school and back, while a student living at a four-year school could get along without a car.
- A community college transfer might have to wait until junior year for some social aspects of a four-year school, such as living apart from parents, having a link to nationally known athletic teams, and joining fraternities and sororities.

Divorce: Spending Less on Splitting Up

Divorce can be life's most traumatic event, but if the decision to split up is final, the process should become a relatively simple business transaction to divvy up assets. But because emotion plays such a large role, divorce can get a lot more complicated—and a lot more expensive—than it needs to be.

About $50 billion a year is spent in North America as a direct result of divorce, according to the Institute for Divorce Financial Analysts. Divorces can range from simple to complex, but saving money largely revolves around two strategies: paying less to your lawyer and paying less to Uncle Sam.

Here are a few ways to avoid wasting money as you navigate the divorce process.

- Cooperate. Working together on any level is far easier said than done because feelings of bitterness and distrust are common. It might even be impossible for especially contentious divorces. Most wasted money stems from emotional decisions, so trying to collaborate will help. Realize you won't get everything you want, which is true of any fair negotiation.
- Limit lawyer bills. Everybody wants a good lawyer to protect his or her interests, but the price of a lawyer is also a factor, especially if the process is unlikely to result in a court battle.

If you have a simple divorce, you might not need a partner in the firm but an associate, who will be less costly. After you hire a lawyer, use him or her sparingly. An attorney should handle court paperwork and lay out your legal rights, duties, and options. If you have few assets and no children, you could use one of the online divorce services to get unhitched for a few hundred dollars.

- Be prepared. Write down questions for your attorney meetings to use the time efficiently. Drawn-out conversations will be billed at the hourly rate of maybe $250 an hour or more. Don't call your lawyer for minor developments. Instead, keep a journal and update your lawyer periodically.

- Use other professionals. Your lawyer is for legal advice. If you need a therapist, by all means, get one. If you need a financial planner, get one. Either will be far better at giving you what you need and far cheaper than billable attorney time. Use your lawyer for only what lawyers can do.

- Use other resources. Library shelves are full of books on divorce, and the Internet has a slew of Web sites, such as www.divorceinfo.com operated by Alabama divorce lawyer Lee Borden. An inexpensive book is *The IDFA Divorce Survival Guide* ($9.95), written by two leaders of the Institute for Divorce Financial Analysts.

- Tax considerations. The old joke is there are three parties to a divorce: the husband, the wife, and the Internal Revenue Service. Cooperating spouses can structure a divorce to pay as little tax as possible, but you might need help from a tax pro. For example, the way you split up stocks that have appreciated by different amounts could have big capital-gains tax consequences. You must decide who receives the child tax deduction and head-of-household tax filing status. You even might try to time your divorce to happen late in the calendar year or early in the next year, depending on the tax impact of filing jointly or as singles. And structuring payments as child support or alimony can have a big tax impact.

- Don't rebound. People who have been in a stagnant marriage sometimes go wild with money, dating every night and spending money frivolously. And if you rebound your way into another marriage, you could be soon facing divorce all over again.

Hospital Bills: Rampant Mistakes Are Sickening

Some hospital charges are outrageously expensive, but many, like the real-life examples given here, are just dead wrong:

- A $1,133 charge for clipping a toenail and sending it to a lab for testing
- A $1,004.50 toothbrush
- $57 for a teddy bear listed as a "cough support device"
- $15 for a bag of ice listed as "thermal therapy"
- $11.20 for a box of tissues listed as a "disposable mucous recovery system"

Health-care billing errors cost consumers big time, with about 5 percent of bills containing "major" errors, according to survey results by *Consumer Reports*. Consumers are spending more than $10 billion a year on overcharges, claims Medical Billing Advocates of America, a self-described patient advocacy group that also sells auditing services through its members.

Overcharges often go undetected because insurance companies routinely pay them through automated bill-payment systems. To their credit, some in the health-care industry, including the American Hospital Association, have begun efforts toward "patient-friendly billing."

But rampant problems remain, and even if you have health insurance, billing mistakes are costing you—through your deductibles and eventually in the form of higher copayments and less coverage.

The first step in making sure you're not overcharged is to get a detailed itemized bill and scrutinize the charges. Here are more tips, some coming with help from hospital bill auditor Nora Johnson, who helps operate Medical Billing Advocates of America.

- Ask whether all the health-care pros are "in-network." Before going in for a scheduled surgery or procedure, make sure all the specialists who will work on you, such as the anesthesiologist or radiologist, are in your insurance network or charge you only in-network rates.

- Track your drugs. Keep a list of drugs administered to you, or have a friend or family member help track them. Be aware you don't have to pay for such over-the-counter supplies as aspirin or an enema, which are part of the hospital's cost of doing business and shouldn't be billed separately.

- Scrutinize emergency procedures. Bills that include an emergency procedure are more likely to have errors. That's because medical personnel working quickly make a priority out of saving the patient first and completing the billing paperwork later. That makes sense, but so does billing you correctly.

- Note weird charges. If the bill notes a circumcision for a baby girl or time for a man in the labor and delivery room, it's a good sign there's something wrong. But you'll only find them if you're looking.

- Look for repetitive charges. If you see multiple X-rays for the same thing, start asking questions. If they took three because of a problem with their equipment or the X-ray didn't turn out right, they can't bill you for the extra one.

- Examine charges for supplies. Hospitals can't charge for tissues, gowns, and other routine supplies, which are part of the room rate. Similarly, operating room supplies, such as gloves, tape, and gauze are included in your per-minute operating room charge. A hospital can't bill separately for it.

- Beware the bundle. Look for terms such as a surgical "tray," "kit," or "pack." Sometimes items within those bundles of supplies are double-billed as separate items. It's even more egregious if they are routine supplies that were already billed as part of the operating room rate, resulting in triple billing.

- Clarify vague charges. Get an itemization of such charges as "lab fees" or "miscellaneous fees" to make sure you're required to pay them.

If you find errors, you can dispute them yourself by contacting the hospital billing department. But don't fully trust a hospital's own billing audit. If you can't get a problem resolved with the hospital, you can get help by contacting the consumer division of your state attorney general's office or hiring an independent medical bill auditor. An auditor is your best bet for finding overcharges, but realize auditors are often paid by keeping 35 percent to 40 percent of whatever overbilled charges they find. Other auditors charge by the hour.

Funerals: Try to Bury the Pain and Guilt

Poor spending decisions often stem from emotions and ignorance. As harsh as it sounds, that's why many people overspend on funerals and burial services. After all, few life events are more emotionally traumatic than death of a loved one. The key as a consumer is to separate your grief from the business transaction of buying funeral and burial products and services. To be clear, being a smart consumer is not about cheaping out on a funeral. It's about providing a dignified farewell without wasting money—money that instead could be used by people still living or by charities, depending on where the estate passes.

Americans annually spend billions of dollars arranging more than two million funerals for family members and friends, according to the Federal Trade Commission. Funerals are among the most expensive purchases consumers will make in their lifetimes. A traditional full-service funeral costs roughly $6,500. Extras can easily push that price past $10,000. Cemetery costs are separate and can add thousands more.

The most helpful, yet morbid, advice stems from this fact: No casket with gaskets, grave liner, burial vault, or any type of embalming will preserve a body indefinitely. Spending extra money trying to preserve a body is a waste.

Funeral spending decisions should be mostly based on family preferences and religious issues, but here are money considerations:

- Compare. In most states, you don't even need to use a funeral home, but assuming that most families probably will use one, know what you're getting into by comparing prices of products and services. Federal regulations require that funeral homes give you price quotes over the phone, so comparing is easy.

- Explore options. Getting the right funeral for the right price is all about examining your choices and not blindly picking a package deal for a "typical" funeral. Funeral homes are required to give you a printed menu of options.

- Realize embalming is optional. Many funeral homes require embalming if you're planning a viewing or visitation. But embalming generally is unnecessary if the body is buried or cremated shortly after death. It is purely for cosmetic purposes. The United States and Canada are the only countries in the world that routinely embalm the dead.

- Forgo the fancy casket. The casket, with its 300% to 500% price markup, is usually the largest expense, ranging from about $2,000 to $10,000. The purpose is to have a decent-looking box to hold the body if there will be a viewing. Ask to see all the models because some funeral directors will at first show you only expensive ones. Or purchase a casket somewhere else, even online, and have it shipped to the funeral home. The funeral director must use it and not charge a fee for using a third-party casket.

- Rent a casket for cremation. Ask about renting a casket for a viewing if the body will be cremated. Eliminate the casket cost altogether if there will be no viewing. No state or local laws require a casket for direct cremations.

- Beware at the cemetery. Unfortunately, federal regulations that protect consumers for funeral purchases do not apply at the cemetery. For example, state laws do not require a vault or liner in the ground to protect the casket. Cemeteries might require them but only because it keeps the ground from settling and makes lawn mowing easier. It has nothing to do with the body. You can shop elsewhere to buy an outer burial container if the cemetery insists on one. The same goes for headstones.

- Plan your own funeral. Much of the stress of making funeral arrangements can be avoided by simply making your wishes known to loved ones. Put your funeral preferences in writing. This does not mean prepaying for a funeral, an idea many experts advise against.

- Learn more. Consumers are protected by federal regulations called "The Funeral Rule." For more information, see a consumer guide by the Federal Trade Commission (FTC) online at www.ftc.gov/bcp/conline/pubs/services/funeral.htm or call 1-877-FTC-HELP. Also see www.funerals.org.

A Final Thought: Buying Happiness

The point of reading this book, assuming you accepted the spending smart philosophy, is to spend less money on things you don't care about so you can spend more on things you do care about.

But what do you care about? Or more importantly, what should you care about? How should you spend your money to derive the greatest happiness?

This is the subject of academic study, and the conclusions are in: It seems we can, in fact, buy happiness. The key is this concept:

Positive life experiences contribute to happiness more than things do.

This point about spending for happiness was well-documented in research by Leaf Van Boven of the University of Colorado at Boulder and Thomas Gilovich at Cornell University. They reported findings in "To do or have? That is the Question," which appeared in the *Journal of Personality and Social Psychology* and later in other academic journal articles. Their research confirmed what literally dozens of other academics had found—that people get more happiness from experiences than material goods. Further, they found that materialistic pursuits—bigger houses, faster cars and the latest electronics—actually erected a barrier to achieving life satisfaction.

Why is this so?

Experiences are more valuable because of mental editing, Van Boven explained to me. The scrapbook in our minds mostly remembers the good parts of experiences, such as vacations. It's not that you completely forget the annoyances; you just remember the joyful events more forcefully. Because of this memory editing, what academics call positive reinterpretation, the experience actually improves with time, like a fine wine.

Think about your favorite memories. If you and your family reminisce about an amusement park outing, you would rarely talk about the long lines or overpriced food but about the fun you had. You barely remember the day it rained on your great beach vacation. Mediocre golfers disregard the many duffs and shanks during a round and instead recall fondly sinking a long putt or hitting a gloriously long drive. A positive memory obliterates in importance the bad shots and keeps the golfer coming back for another round.

By contrast, material purchases mostly lose value as they age, both in monetary worth and how much we appreciate them. You likely will never be more thrilled with a material purchase than during the first few days you own it. It's downhill from there.

Some people prefer material possessions because they have something tangible to show for their money. They fail to recognize that memories of experiences are durable and every bit as valuable as something you can touch.

Here are tips to get the most out of your experience dollars:

- Set goals. Imagine yourself at the end of your life and looking back. On your deathbed, would you regret not buying the latest iPod music player or spending more quality time with your children and friends? Or, to use a collective American experience, put yourself in the mind-set of the days following the Sept. 11, 2001, terrorist attacks. What seemed important then?

Most people would value experiences more than the possessions, but it's easy to lose perspective in daily living and spending. So write down your values and goals, and ways to achieve them. The list will not only give you a road map for spending your money, but also spending your time.

- Include people. Do as many enjoyable activities with other people as you can. Including others is a fundamental component to a truly happy experience.

- Don't overspend. On a happiness scale, you don't necessarily get what you pay for with experiences. It has far more to do with the quality of time spent with other people than how extravagant or luxurious the experience is.

Spending smarter can free up money. And money can buy episodes of happiness. The key is to spend discretionary money on doing, rather than owning.

Learn more about spending smart online at www.gregkarp.com.

INDEX

W-X-Y-Z

FINANCIAL TIMES

In an increasingly competitive world, it is quality
of thinking that gives an edge—an idea that opens new
doors, a technique that solves a problem, or an insight
that simply helps make sense of it all.

We work with leading authors in the various arenas
of business and finance to bring cutting-edge thinking
and best-learning practices to a global market.

It is our goal to create world-class print publications
and electronic products that give readers
knowledge and understanding that can then be
applied, whether studying or at work.

To find out more about our business
products, you can visit us at www.ftpress.com.